The Freemason

Johann Baptist Krebs

The Freemason

Johann Baptist Krebs

translated by Kerry A Nitz

The right to publish the essence of the royal art, masonry, to introduce it practically into life, rests on a necessity which every true brother must fall into line with who feels the urge for it. But called are those for whom life is more than a vegetative process. — Thou thousands may at any rate only honour the form, seeking fearfully to banish the spirit — in the light of humanity, he should, must, and will still prosper happily and bring ample fruit, and in him the noblest amongst humanity gather and also recognise him in bourgeois life as a brother — then the pure gold is freed of its dross, and the masonry is what it should be, a world alliance which encompasses all, even if only isolated ones achieve masterhood. —

K A Nitz
WHANGANUI, NEW ZEALAND

Der Freimaurer
first published in German 1844
under the pseudonym J. B. Kerning

This translation into New Zealand English
from the third edition of 1879
Copyright © K A Nitz 2024
All rights reserved

ISBN: 978-0-473-72398-9

Table of Contents

Translator's Note

For the English translation of Bible texts I have made use of the King James Version. Where I thought it would be helpful I have also inserted missing Biblical citations in the footnotes.

The occasionally somewhat idiosyncratic approach of the author to presenting dialogue has also been retained in part.

***

Forward
to the First Edition

Freemasonry cannot continue to exist with honour without the surveillance of the world. As much as its disciples endeavour to hide their activities, the great public knows though that it does not possess the proper unity in its striving. In order to prevent all false judgements, the author has undertaken, without though publishing the ceremonial, to give the world a description of the essential gradations, not discrepancies, of freemasonry in order to put everyone who reads this in a position to judge unbiasedly over the activity of any system, even any lodge, and to recognise from its fruits the aim of its activities.

Everywhere freemasonry, even when it concerns itself only with the social goals of humanity, works beneficently; only it must, in so far as its effects apply to humanity, not be an isolated limb of it, else it expels itself and becomes, instead of twining itself more and more around the whole, a species which acts without any generality and only expresses in its halls what it should in actual fact be practising.

We seek the truth and therefore must not deceive the world. But we deceive it when we claim we are one in goal and handling. According to the goal we are indeed one, in so far as we walk on one and the same path, only in the distance to the goal great variation reigns. A part strives for the furthest goal, for the others the close lying goal is already sufficient. Anyone who strives to reach the furthest goal must nevertheless pass through the close lying one, meanwhile those who suffice with

9

the close one often have no idea about the furthest, the highest goal. Regardless of this all freemasons consider each other to be brothers because they are united at the beginning of the path, then urge forwards as far as free will or courage and strength allow. The steps of the forward striving are in this work indicated according to the experiences made by the author, and he asks the reader to take them precisely to heart and to judge freemasonry according to this yardstick according to which its disciples are required already with the first step on the path called upon to seek ennoblement and perfection of their nature in that they place the purest seeds of humanity into their hearts.

Where humanity prevails, there is the spirit of God. Where love reigns, there the power of creation rejoices because love is the principle of all being and becoming. Well now, so go outward, you lines of this book, awaken hearts to humanity and love, and if you achieve this only to some extent, then your goal is fulfilled, and I may not rue having sent you out.

Stuttgart, January 1841.

The Author.

***

Foreword
to the Third Edition

Almost four decades have passed since the present text was published by its long since passed away author. But still today the same reasons as are laid out in the foreword to the first edition apply to having the book makes its way out for a third time. And it may be seen as a gratifying sign that in our very turbulent days reading of this type is also sought.

With affectionate piety, with sparing hand, and with open eyes, one has endeavoured to provide the text in a formal direction with the necessary improvements. Materially nothing was changed at all.

May this deeply earnest discussion of the long since departed win many new friends! May his memory be offered by this new edition of his book a thankful homage!

Stuttgart, January 1879.

***

Part 1: Christianity

Truly, the teachings of Christ are words of eternal wisdom,
They raise to God he who dedicates his heart to them.

Introduction

The main person of these pages, Johann Friedrich Gomphardt — whose parents were torn from him by death before he had finished boyhood, but who had later received through the care of his uncle a thoroughly scientific education — took over in his twenty-fifth year the self-administration of his inheritance of a significant landed estate and was looking around, in order to have someone to share his spirit and heart with, a life companion whom he soon found, and indeed in a way that he could reckon himself in this respect amongst the numbers of the most fortunate.

Amalie Ruppert, daughter of a banker, taken in to be raised by an aunt in Hamburg because of the early death of her parents, seemed by virtue of her talents entirely made for the great world; only her heart drew her constantly out into the open air and into the gardens where she occupied herself with plants and often discussed with the gardener the most expedient manner for dealing with this or that branch of gardening. For this reason she visited, as often as she obtained permission, a relative in Gl., a small country town which lay only an hour's distance from Gomphardt's estate. It was here that he got to know her, and since everything which he saw and heard about her agreed with his way of thinking and feeling, he asked for her hand and introduced her three months later as co-owner in a well-arranged country house.

As you would have foreseen, so it was — the new couple were outwardly happy, for each of them endeavoured to increase the contentment of the other and thereby to establish their own happiness all the more certainly. Only one sorrow crept occasionally into their quiet conversations — they were childless. This thought sometimes cast a cloud over the outpourings of the husband's and wife's hearts. But mutual respect and love shooed away any bitterness from them, and thus they lived, for the joy of each other and as example to others, in an agreement that is seldom seen.

Ten years flowed by in lovely happiness, and the thought of having no children had already long since lost the power of any saddening effect. But what joy when one day Amalie revealed to her husband that she felt herself to be in a state whereby her life's happiness would achieve the highest peak and each of her wishes would find satisfaction.

To describe Gomphardt's bliss over this discovery would be an attempt made in vain. He exulted and poured tears at the same time and would at that moment have disseminated his happiness amongst his people and neighbours if his wife had not held him back. But the next day he was already beginning to make arrangements which let a future son and heir be suspected without a great gift for decipherment. "If it is a boy," he often said enthusiastically, "then I will no longer lack anything for making life into a paradise."

The time passed amidst wishes, dreams, and hopes. The decisive day arrived, but soon indicated dangerous symptoms. Through the help of the long since ordered doctor, who called on all that art and science was capable of, finally a dead little boy appeared. Deep silence reigned. The woman who had just given birth lay unconscious, wavering between life and death. You did not know what you should wish or hope for.

The child, in order to escape the sight of the mother in case she awoke, was taken into another room. All eyes were directed to her, still lying in a deep unconscious state, in anxious expectation. Finally she opened her eyes and looked around anxiously; but since she seemed not to become aware of what she sought, she made a forceful motion and fell loudly groaning back into the previous daze.

Gomphardt was barely capable of holding onto himself. "Save my wife," he said to the doctor and those present; "the loss of the child I will bear."

Everything was now directed to calling the wife back to life. After three hours of anxious efforts she came to, looked around, like the first time, with searching eyes, and when she espied nothing, when nobody stirred to satisfy the wish to be read in her eyes, she cried out in anguish, "My child is dead!"

"Get a hold of yourself!", Gomphardt said. "You are alive. Get a hold of yourself and survive for me; otherwise I will not be able to live anymore either." She looked at him with indescribable emotion and endeavoured to reach her hand out to him. "The child is dead!", she now stammered; "God has taken it to himself before I could see it. I will soon follow him, I feel it." — "No," Gomphardt wailed, "You will live and be happy through my love."

She looked at him with rigid eyes, meanwhile her breast rose struggling and her breathing got worse. Gomphardt placed his hand on her upper abdomen as if he wanted to calm her thereby. She slung her arm around his, closed her eyes and fell asleep calmly. No attempt was made to awaken her. "Nature demands its rights," the doctor said; "perhaps some strengthening will occur from the rest." Everybody left the room, only Gomphardt remained with her and listened for each of her breaths.

This state had lasted two hours when she awoke seemingly a little strengthened. Her eyes, however, were still unsteady and swayed inquiringly from one side to the other as if something must show itself to her. With the entrance of the doctor, who wanted to check on her again, she was indeed startled, only she looked him sharply in the eye as if she wanted to read his soul. He soothed her and said, "You have slept. Take this for a good sign! Rest is the best medicine against such a violent commotion as you were put into. We want to use nothing for the time being except tempering means and let your good nature prevail." He left to visit some patients in the neighbourhood, with the promise to return again in a short time and to see what further was to be done.

The doctor appeared after night had already fallen, and found the patient again in such a calm slumber that you would have believed the worst would now have been overcome. Regardless of that he decided to wait until she had awoken, in order to finally hear once more finally from her something about the state of her health. Towards midnight she awoke and began to speak, but with a weak voice. At the question of the doctor about how it was going, she answered, aside from the pressure on her chest which was making her breathing difficult, she felt quite well. A medicine had already been prepared in advance to hinder the rush of the blood and to treat the fever. She took it punctually all night, and the next morning you could have hoped confidently for her rising.

Had in the moment of awakening and clear consciousness the pain over the loss of her child not won the upper hand with her so much, nature, art, and care would certainly have won and have restored her; but when you consider that ailments of the soul can make even the healthiest person ill, you must not be astonished if the doctor gave up almost all hope after two days and only saw a faint outlook of rescue in the punctual following of his prescriptions and in the fortunate and undisturbed working together of the life powers.

Gomphardt crept about like a corpse. He sought hope in the eyes of everyone who had to be about the patient for her care. Then he plucked up courage, went himself to her to seek solace and only left her again in order not to alarm her with his anguish.

Thus it lasted six days. The state of the illness indeed did not improve, but also did not seem to get worse. When the doctor appeared on the seventh day and checked the pulse of the patient, his face clouded at once, and all those present who became aware of it were startled in the most violent way. He went with Gomphardt into another room to prepare him and to ask him to prepare for the worst because his wife would only survive the coming day with difficulty. Gomphardt's anguish over this and the sympathy of everyone in the house for the impending loss is not to be described. Enough, towards evening the deciding crisis occurred. An hour before sunset the patient seemed to be struggling enormously in her inner-being, so that you would think the thread of her life would now break — only by and by she became calm and for the first time during the illness amiable and talkative. Gomphardt, the doctor, and also the clergyman, the Deacon, who had already been visiting frequently during the illness, but could never speak with her, were present. She inquired after everything, especially after a few of her servants and asked, in the case that she died, that they not be turned out. In accordance with her wish to see then those whom she had to thank for especial kindness, a quite large company gathered about her in her room. She spoke with each and expressed feelings of thanks. But she turned to the Deacon with the following words, "You have made the effort to guide me on the path to God, to eternity. Unfortunately I was a slow pilgrim. The happiness which I enjoyed in the love of my husband and many faithful souls often led me to not hear your words. Now I am required to walk quickly; hence guide me so that I do not stumble."

The Deacon, who had been counted amongst the friends of the house for many years, replied full of emotion, "Your way of walking, dear friend, I can by my apostolic conviction call nothing but praiseworthy. You have sowed love and received love. Poverty did not have to seek first, not knock first on your door; everywhere where help was expedient and necessary, it was provided by you, often without knowing how and from where. You have loved the church, never neglected it, and thereby set a beautiful example that one with all the earthly riches also has eternal goods to gather. The time of pilgrimage was used faithfully from your side; may the entry into eternity, whether it follows now or in later years, lead you to the throne of the father, to the original source of love whose spirit led you up to now and placed love of humanity, charity, and every Christian virtue in your soul."

These words seemed to have strengthened her noticeably. "Thank you", she replied, "for the solace which you give me. Even in this hour I reproach myself for having though so seldom thought of your teachings and of God. I was too happy, so inexpressibly happy, that I often endeavoured in vain to express it. If God can look less mercifully on a fortune which you recognise as such than on a misfortune, then I must give up hope. But if the thankfulness which I constantly felt, if the struggles I fought for a few days, are also placed on the scales, then I hope to find a balancing out, if not also with the eternal justness, then with the eternal love. Only one thing unsettles me, over one doubt I find no solace in the infinite goodness of

God — my child is dead! Can or will God call it into life for my sake?"

The Deacon was a little embarrassed by this question; his ardent wish to console, but principally the inexhaustibility of Biblical grounds for solace gave his mouth words of edification, and he consoled her thus, "The power of the Christian religion is great, and anyone who has trust in it builds on solid ground. Your child is in God's hands, dead for this world; but there the breath of life can animate it for a purer life course. Indeed the thought that what here came into the world dead will nonetheless live in the hereafter is incomprehensible to earthly understanding; only who can set a bound on the eternal love and say up to here it works and no further? The saviour himself, when the apostles asked him whether this or that would also continue to live and arrive in heaven, answered that according to human wisdom, no, but for the grace of the father anything is possible. In this grace we want in our case to trust, and since it is infinite, it will not let a mother's heart live in want, a heart which is indeed the purest and most untainted reflection of the eternal love."

She thanked the worthy consoler with inexpressible emotion and said, "How whole I am with the knowledge which you give me! My child lives, it must live through my love and the infinite love of God who created us all for the happiness of love. If it comes as it will, I am ready to confidently subject myself to his will."

She fell silent. A silence reigned for about two minutes, as if death had already opened his terrible basket. But now she began anew, while she sought to grasp Gomphardt's hand, and said, "How much I love and have loved you, God alone knows. Now I will part from you." — Gomphardt wanted to speak, but she did not let him get any words out and continued, "Do not console me and yourself in vain! The hour of parting has arrived. Do not grumble and just think what God does is well done. I go ahead and will wait there with our child for you. The hereafter is the land where no separation is possible anymore. There, if it is possible, a yet more intimate love will connect us; there no sorrow and no death will sadden us, and what our souls began here, they will continue without interruption and end. Take a hold of yourself! The judge approaches — I am being collected — our saviour of all — will — lead me to the father."

She spoke the last words, syllable for syllable, slower and slower, opened her eyes upward once more, and passed away.

The doctor said with wavering voice, "She has died." — The Deacon raised his hands and prayed, "God take her into the kingdom of your saints." — Gomphardt fell down at her side, clasped the bed firmly and whimpered and lamented so that they began to be anxious about him. The Deacon sought to console him, he did not hear him. All those present asked him to pull himself together. He said forcibly, "I do not want to pull myself together. I have lost everything, and hence I want only to live my anguish and seek nothing else than what can increase it."

They relented from trying to get through to him, only they arranged to not leave him alone and to make sure to protect him from violence against himself.

The Funeral

After they could only push Gomphardt with effort the next day to remove himself from the dead woman and to go to his room in order to not be a hindrance to the women preparing her body, the Deacon came to inquire for himself after his state of health. Gomphardt barely deigned to answer him and said with muted voice, "For me everything is dead." The worthy clergyman approached him and said with hearty insistence, "You have lost much, and it would be of little help to want to make the greatness of your loss smaller than it is. No! By us seeking to acknowledge the perfect virtues of the one who has passed, we prepare ourselves the most certain solace and strengthen our heart with feelings of love for a higher world ahead to which she has indeed gone, but yet remains connected with us in the closest way."

Gomphardt, who seemed not to hear what the Deacon was saying, raised his gaze and said, "You are a worthy clergyman! You have accepted me from time immemorial with amiable and paternal care! Even now in misfortune you do not abandon me. If something could console me, then it would be the certainty that a soul still lives which shares in my destiny. Only the love for my wife is so closely intertwined with the history of my inner-being that I still cannot foresee how I will live without her."

The Deacon did not stop trying to get through to him and portraying to him the necessity of getting a hold of himself. To achieve this end all the more certainly, he asked him to lie down and to strengthen himself with the refreshing sleep for which he had already long done without. — Gomphardt did not want to agree to that to start with, but finally he gave in to the repeated requests and lay down, indeed in his clothes, on a bed which was in the room, where he fell into a deep sleep already after a few minutes.

He continued to sleep for three hours. When he awoke and saw himself in such an unusual position, the entire weight of his loss at once fell on his soul again. He went to the room of his wife to inquire whether he could not yet see her. They put him off for an hour. Meanwhile the sexton had also arrived to inquire about when and in what manner the burial should take place. Gomphardt felt forcibly shocked by this inquiry and responded by asking whether nobody else could take over this decision. The sexton told him to bear in mind that Mr Gomphardt himself must decide over it, because nobody else would get involved for fear of doing too much or too little. "Well," Gomphardt said, "then I will order grave and coffin, will do everything to give her body back to the earth from which it was gathered for me as the most precious of flowers which can delight mortals and which was rooted so deeply in my heart."

He immediately strode to work, had all those who were occupied in such a case receive the necessary instructions and sent messengers to his friends and acquaintances in the neighbourhood in order to inform them of his mourning. Meanwhile the body had been dressed and placed on a daybed in the living room of the departed for compassionate friends to view. Gomphardt, who had been notified of it, went there, saw her before himself like a sleeping saint and had trouble keeping himself upright. Now he stepped up to her, grasped her cold hand, and shuddered. "She is dead," he stammered; "such stiff coldness must not approach life! She is dead and does not see and hear my lament." Now he fell silent, sat down by her on a chair, and did not leave her side the entire day.

The next day visitors came to whom he had to devote himself; the remaining arrangements also occupied him in so many ways that he only obtained a few moments of time in which to see the departed. And thus it continued until the day of the funeral. — —

The moment when the coffin accepts the shell of a beloved being and is then closed remains for those left behind always the most distressing; but if you have already seen how the dead body by and by is becoming earth-like, the feeling of the necessity of such a treatment merges with the pain, and you endure what you previously barely dared to think. Thus too here. Gomphardt shook when the dear shell was withdrawn from his sight, only he retained the strength to bear it and to be present at the act of burial with a steadfastness which astonished all who had previously been concerned about him. "It has happened," he said when the Deacon, arriving with him at the house, sought to still console him. "It has happened," he repeated; "she is gone and will never return. I cannot change it and must endure it." The Deacon replied, "So speaks the man whose eyes gaze outwards, who submits to the counsel of God. I will leave you, but ask you to allow me to visit you daily in order to draw the conviction from your mouth that noble hearts do not give up hope." Gomphardt thanked him and asked him to fulfil his promise because only he knew the virtues of the departed and knows how great the wound is which the death struck to his heart.

The Deacon left. The residents of the house went about their usual business, and Gomphardt was now left alone.

The Deacon visited him every day punctually, but his utterances, as soon as the talk turned to serious life circum-stances, had too apostolic a character for Gomphardt's simple disposition and seldom gave the reinforcement which he needed. "My happiness", he said once after such a conversat-ion, "alienated me from humanity, they do not understand me and I do not understand them anymore. But in order to put you, dear Deacon, in a state to be able to judge my position properly, I will ask you to listen to a short outline of my youth and my course of education; then your magnanim-ity will excuse me for having abandoned myself to the anguish in an unmanly way.

You know that I had lost my parents already as a boy. — In boyhood you seldom learn to properly appreciate the worth of being guided by father and mother. They died, and I cried because others did, genuinely, but the impression which they imagined I was seized by, I did not feel. Only when I became more mature and arrived at university did I feel how much I missed compared to others. When my comrades visited their parents during the holidays, I went to the house of my uncle, who made a conscientious accounting over my expenditure, but did not welcome me with his heart full of love. I had several other relatives, and it seemed to me often as if they distributed me amongst themselves during the holidays so that each should take part in the burden of catering for me for a few weeks without being allowed to calculate compensation for it. The university life too, which so many still consider in old age to be the most beautiful time of their earthly life, gave me no opportunity to awaken the feelings of my heart and to give them a specific direction. Since I studied neither jurisprudence, nor medicine, nor theology, and consequently belonged to no faculty, I could not easily connect with student societies or other associations and remained in this way almost left to myself, which state I used for my studies in such a way that I learnt more in *one* year than many other learn in three. Natural history, world history, philosophy, maths, government administration, agriculture, and alongside these the study of old languages were the subjects which I took up with earnest, and in them I made such progress that you might have believed I would dedicate myself completely in the future to scholarship and deal with these branches theoretically and publicly. Only despite my love for the sciences I could barely await the time of my majority in order to escape the city life and to gratify in the open air of nature feelings which I had often felt forebodingly in my inner-being without being able to give a name to them. The time of my minority finally passed. I came here, looked around for a wife at first, without actually knowing why, and heaven led me, as if it wanted to make good all the previous neglect, to a being who was father, mother, sibling, and wife for me, who first taught me what living meant, who united in herself everything which can raise and delight humans, who made me, in a word, into a human. And now, since Amalie has raised me up, since she awoke in me the capability for the most beautiful ennoblement and perfecting of my nature, now, when I could repay her, she is torn from me, and I must sink back into the night again from which she had freed me, and see myself delivered to a blind, heartless fate. Before I knew my wife, my life was a meaningless dream which left behind not the slightest reality. With her it obtained sense and meaning because my heart came alive. Now I stand alone again, the sun of life has gone down for me, and hence I find no hold on the future; hence I cannot yet think how I will be able to live without her."

The Deacon had listened to this story with great attentiveness. After its end he rose from his seat, walked back and forth a few times through the room thoughtfully and said, as he stopped before Gomphardt, the following.

"Your story, without containing anything special, is of such a peculiar sort that one is only with the assistance of it put in a state to judge your loss and your state of mood properly. But be reassured! The means of being able to evaluate the worth of your late wife so comprehensively will also lend you the power to learn to comprehend the worth of life overall all the more distinctly. She has passed on, we will follow her and accomplish there what we began here. Do not free yourself of the feeling of mourning! It is now necessary for you; only realise that you dispose through the satisfaction of this need with a sacred debt which, the more cleanly it is discharged, then the more refreshing it must be. Mourning is needed, is in the present case a fruit of love; but if it becomes too powerful, if it threatens to dominate us entirely, then it is a rampant plant which draws all the material sustenance around it to itself and destroys the nobler seeds. Immoderate mourning can lead to hardness, to hate of humanity and divert us from the path of love on which alone the memory of a dear departed can be worthily celebrated."

Gomphardt seemed to become perceptibly calmer at these words. He said, "You are right, Deacon! Mourning is a fruit of love, and as such it should not work destructively, but rather beneficially. Since where love was, now mourning reigns, and in so far as this mourning is also love, it should be pleasant to me and keep me connected with Amalie. Thank you for this solace and I see now for the first time how rich your disposition must be in noble feelings, since you are in a position to touch the strings which the mourner often believes they hear alone. You have there touched the innermost and most melodious strings of my heart, I will listen to their sound with quiet devotion and thereby obtain a resignation which no academic philosophy would be in a position to give me."

The Deacon rejoiced over this turn in the mood of his friend, and after he had added a few words for the reinforcement of that mood, he parted with the blissful consciousness of having faithfully fulfilled his profession of consoling the sad.

***

The Resignation

Gomphardt's further mourning, his brooding and his indecisiveness in everything which he undertook in the initial period will be passed over here as not relevant to the matter. He abandoned himself to the impressions of his feelings; wherever these drew him, he nourished them with images of memories from the times of his happiness. For this reason he occupied himself for a few days with the estate of his wife and finally had everything brought to his room for a more comfortable perusal. In a casket he found amongst accounts, letters, and books also her diary which she had kept in the house of her aunt, in which it had not taken a turn for the best for her, and had written down all her feelings in it. At the start of it, it read: "The human heart must be able to express itself, to confide. Since I find here no soul of the same stamp, you, little book, shall be my friend to whose interior I will entrust my thoughts and feelings."

Gomphardt felt wonderfully seized by this idea and said, "Yes, Amalie, you are right, the human heart must be able to express itself, to confide, otherwise it is a light whose beams find no focus and lose themselves without trace. Amalie! You were, when you reigned in my house, my model and teacher; even now you are still it! Your noble disposition felt the need to express itself, and since human hearts were not available to you, this book sufficed for you. I will follow your example and write down in my own diary my thoughts and feelings in order to at least hear myself and get to know my wishes, hopes, and doubts."

He examined yet other books and writings from her hand and finally found a book of which, still quite new and blank, the title contained simply: accounts book for unspecified, but obligatory expenditure! "What should this title signify?", Gomphardt continued reflecting. "Unspecified, but obligatory expenditure! — Can there be such a thing? And how can the unspecified be obligatory? That I cannot ask her! How beautifully she would interpret it! — She did not live only for the cold, already determined laws, but also for those which were written in her heart, and which must be brought into practice everywhere the moment demands it. This book shall be my law book; in it I will ask myself what are laws of the heart and what are commandments of cold reason."

The examination of the objects before him had occupied him so much that evening had arrived before he realised. He had the supper brought to him, then sorted everything again and went to bed, firmly resolved to set to work from that morning on without any interruption at his intention to keep a diary.

The next day nothing relevant occurred. But when in the evening everybody had withdrawn from work, Gomphardt sat down at his writing desk and began, as he had given himself the promise, to write down with honest frankness his feelings and thoughts.

W. the 12th October.

Eight days after the burial of my dear above all unforgettable wife, I undertake to establish for myself a diary in which I will express everything which occurs to my feelings and understanding.

From feelings and understanding arises the human; and even if now my feelings are predominant, there is yet the opportunity for the understanding to contemplate much of what it would have to lack in a calm state of mind.

Feeling reigns; but the understanding walks alongside as critic and hinders it from going astray.

Feeling loses its way when it abandons the course of love, forgets good deeds received, even turns hostilely towards the benefactor. Along such false paths I cannot stray so long as I think of you, Amalie. If this memory may fill me also with sorrow and pain, then sorrow and pain are testimony of the love, of the thanks and the acknowledgement of all that which you were to me and have done for me, they are still kindnesses to me. Yes, Amalie, you were my everything, and as I write here, I am speaking with you and deceive my heart lovingly in order to give it a few moments of rest so as to be able to mourn all the more intimately again my loss.

Indeed they say feeling and thinking are two disparate things. Feelings, they claim, cannot think and so the natural stage of animal life which does not rise above instinct is thereby allocated to them. Those who speak in such a way do not know love, have never truly loved, otherwise they would have to know that the feeling of a pure love possesses a sort of omniscience before which the finest logic must fall silent — and that it speaks a language against which the phrases of many poets and scholars are only vague intimations. The feelings of humans are of a higher nature; from them arises the means to think. Anyone who cannot feel humanly is also incapable of thinking, hence I will live for the feeling and believe what it says to me and be strengthened by the act.

13th October.

Here I am again in order to talk with you, Amalie, again.

You were and I am!

You were! How horridly this idea penetrates through all the nerves of my body and almost makes the marrow in my bones ossify. You were, the senses say; you are, the feelings say. Whom may I believe?

I have resolved to constantly believe and obey my feelings. But are the perceptions of the senses not also feelings? — If the eyes say: I do not see — the ear: I do not hear — is there then yet a feeling which can maintain: you also see without seeing, you hear without hearing? Feelings are of a practical nature; what they do not stimulate, what does not act on them, is not present for them. Amalie! Your flown image lives still in me, still acts on me! Is this sufficient to say irrefutably: you are, you live still?

Who places these questions to me? The understanding or the feelings?

The understanding knows nothing but that it was said to it that the soul continues to live after death. The feelings wish for the continued existence, and hence they are so mightily seized by the outlook of it. The understanding defines and regards the definition as higher than the thing itself. The feelings want to live, but desire, so as to fully reassure themselves, factual proof.

Where have I got to? I am setting up a desire which can never be realised. The feelings are working here in an abyss from which they see no hope of being freed. Formerly, yes formerly, as the holy scripture teaches, the dead returned and gave knowledge about their continued existence. Can what formerly happened not also still happen now? — Amalie! I am trembling as I write this. Amalie! You could release the doubt which oppresses me, could tell me whether you only were or whether you still are!

What desires are rising in me? Is it then possible to doubt here where the entire world seems to believe! Who can fight against the doubts when they come? They are like the sandflies in summer; who may shoo these away?

The priest says religion vanquishes all doubt. He says! But do we well know whether he doubts himself? — What he teaches occurs from his official duty; of his doubts he does not have to give any account. Amalie! You could free me from the uncertainty in which I am wavering.

I must not follow these thoughts any further, otherwise I will end up in a labyrinth from which there is no exit anymore. Amalie! Why have you left me? Why must I enter through your death a situation where I become doubtful of God and immortality?

14th October.

I am alone! This consciousness presses me almost to the ground. I was at your grave and would have liked to have dug it up in order to descend to you. — Death, you are terrible, are the robber of all happiness and make all of nature around us into a mortuary. Why are you in creation? Who gives you the power to dissolve the most sacred feelings of life and to make them stiffen in your cold arms? Does then no eternal love reign in nature? Does it possess no force to scare you off when you stretch out your hand towards connected hearts? I must almost doubt in an eternal love because you may separate creatures who swore eternal loyalty and were happy through loyalty! Eternal love! Can you tolerate it that death breaks into your property and desecrates the purest feelings? Eternal love! I become uncertain of you, become uncertain of everything which was otherwise sacred to me, and struggle in a terrible battle where no hope of a victory waves to me. Oh, eternal love, if you exist, do not let me fall away from you, so that through the belief in you I retain strength to eke out my life and not go under shamefully.

You — no, not you, death has torn everything from me, but you have not hindered it from committing the theft! Does that agree with the concept of an infinite love? No, it does not agree, and hence I would, if I had not loved and yet loved, have to despair of love.

I must not express myself further. I see that I am committing an outrage; but my heart, my feelings drive me to it, and what these say should indeed be the truth. Amalie! Were you only, or are you still! I could console myself if I knew for certain that you still live! But through my wretched doubt any outlook of solace has been taken completely from me, and I stand like someone lost who has lost any hope of finding the way out of the desert.

15th October.

Here I sit again before my mirror. But the images which it shows me are more shocking than attractive.

It is something else to keep a diary in which you write down unbiasedly the inputs and outputs and the incidental events of the day, than instead your feelings and thoughts, whatever sort they might be too. The former has no moral influence; the latter, however, is a sort of God's judgement where weakness and outrage stand next to one another, in whose midst the truth sits at court with incorruptible scales and speaks the judgement to our inner-being.

Truth, they say, is the most perfect thing in creation. Does truth stand above love? Can they not go hand in hand? Dark path on which I arrive once more! Shall I then not find any point of light anymore?

Love has wounded my heart fatally; can truth heal this wound? For me there is only *one* truth, to know whether Amalie lives. If that is so, then love is the truth, and I walk on its path. If love is not truth, then I must seek another path and deceive myself as much as possible about the time of my existence.

One means, there is just *one* in all of creation, which could satisfy me. I have never clearly expressed it from lack of courage. Faintheartedness in a shattered heart is negative truth, for it is what it should not be. But courage remains under all circumstances a virtue and to be incapable of being virtuous from faintheartedness dishonours us before ourselves, and all claims to reality are lost. I will pluck up courage and express my desires on whose fulfillment or non-fulfilment the direction of my future life depends. Amalie! To you who was everything to me, whose image I bear in my heart, to you I turn and implore:

Look across to me from the unknown hereafter! Penetrate through the grave, show and give me a certainty that you still live. In ancient times the dead left their graves and showed themselves to those left behind. With the glorification of Christ those already long dead stepped out from their narrow dwelling and announced to pious souls the resurrection from the dead. Not through splendid doctrines, but through witnesses from the hereafter does the eternal love strengthen despondent hearts. I too am despondent, I too need the strengthening, and who can give it to me more willingly and convincingly than you who is bound to me through bonds of the most intimate love. Amalie! Give me your testimony, let me see, hear, or feel you, but so that no doubt in the reliability of your revelation is possible anymore, then my belief in an eternal love, in God and immortality will receive such a strength that nothing more will be in a position to shake it. If you do not grant my request, then I will sink into the night of an unbelief in which no light illuminates a higher truth and the sunshine of any hope vanishes.

I close off here and remain yours, Amalie, by day and night. This book will remain unused for as long as until I know whether you will hear me or not. Amalie, come, come to me so that I do not despair in God and the eternity of life through the certainty of having lost you forever!

He closed the writing desk and pleaded, before he went to bed, for the fulfillment of his wish. In the morning, before he went about his business, he did the same, and thus for seven weeks without, however, receiving the slightest enlightenment. During this time he became more and more earnest and taciturn so that the Deacon considered it his duty to visit him and make him explain himself.

***

The Unbelief

The Deacon did not hesitate for long in his intentions and paid a visit the very next day to Gomphardt. He sought to make the introduction as simple as possible, to investigate the state of mind of the latter, and to offer him, if he needed it, the balm of solace. Gomphardt received him obligingly, listened to the cause of his visit calmly, and said, "Deacon, I know your sympathy for my fate and will uncover the depths of my heart to you and keep nothing unsaid which goes on in it.

You have seen how the unexpected death of my wife shook me, how I sought solace and strove to hold fast to any shimmer of it, even if only for moments. My dejection finally was also joined by doubt over whether she lives, whether I will see her again. Whoever knows then what the suffering of the soul is will comprehend my state. Robbed of the happiness which had penetrated my entire being, incapable of finding lasting solace anywhere, I turned my gaze to the hereafter in order to strengthen myself in the outlook of seeing her again, then this darkened too. I thought about the ways and at the same time about the possibility of her continued existence and lost touch in the end with every thread which had connected me with the future, and saw myself at the point of having to tell myself, 'There is no life after death — there is no reunion!'"

The Deacon was very shocked at these words. "Dear Gomphardt", he said, "what talk has slipped out of your mouth? No life after death! No freedom after the pressure of time! No state of light after the necessary transformation from the earthly into the spiritual where our true life first begins! — My friend, banish such thoughts and do not sur-render to a deadening unbelief which, in that it clouds the present, obstruct us from the entrance to a happy future."

Gomphardt did not know what answer he should give. His natural good-naturedness restrained him from hurting the Deacon through contradicting him, and yet he could not win himself over to feigning a belief which had so completely left him. Finally he said, "Deacon! Do not become indignant over a confession which I considered it to be my duty to make to you. In so far as you possess means to liberate me from the burden of my unbelief, then share them with me! You will find willing ears, and even if I see only a shimmer of hope, a receptive disposition. But forgive me if I do not feign it. The doctor who does not know the illness of his patient will not bring about his health. Consider yourself to be a doctor and me as the patient which you have in your care, and count on my deepest thanks if you succeed in curing me."

The face of the Deacon became noticeably more cheerful at these assurances. "You are giving me hope once again", he continued confidently. "The patient who subjects himself so willingly to the cure has already won much, and if your good nature, that is here if your heart comes to our assistance, then the result can be nothing other than favourable. But since your confession surprised me so much, begrudge me time to think about the ways of treating you and over the means to be used. I will leave you now and promise to see you again tomorrow, if a visit so soon is not a burden to you, and to begin the work of healing which you yourself have demanded of me."

Gomphardt had again been opening his diary since a few days before and continued expressing his feelings and thoughts with the greatest unbiasedness in it. Today, when everything seemed to have been left in peace and a fleeting snow flurry was whispering at the windows, he sat down at his writing desk and poured himself out in the following way.

23rd December.

What I am, I do not know — for what I am destined, just as little. Some say humans belong to time, others to eternity.

Time and eternity! Through what means are they to be distinguished! Can time exist without eternity and eternity without time? Time is a section of eternity, consequently contained in the former. Eternity is, however, a sequence of sections of time which are always renewing themselves, giving birth to themselves again and again, and thus continuing into eternity. The human is born in time and dies in it. The small section which he forms in the book of eternity begins in the cradle and ends in the grave. After the section has come to an end, can a new one follow with the same content? That would be certainly against all order though. The human is a creature of the senses; all feelings and thoughts occur to him through external impressions; if the outer organs decay, all activity of the feelings and of understanding stops, and the course is at an end. Thus nature teaches us, thus reason and thus the silence of eternity which remains silent to our petitions and complaints and does not dignify us with any information. Amalie! I have turned to you, you would have informed me if you still lived; your love would not have abandoned me in the gruesomest struggle which humans can battle. Amalie! There is still time, you can still break the crust of unbelief which has drawn about my heart and reconcile me with eternal love. Oh come! I am calling you again, and give me me that informative solace of seeing you again!

***

The next day the Deacon arrived and, after the usual greetings were over and both had taken their seats, began his work of conversion with the following words.

"The apostolic faith is a light which illuminates all who confess to the Christian religion and are taken up through the holy sacraments into its church. This faith is the power of creation of eternal life which nourishes itself through hope and prepares in us a rebirth pervaded by love, a rebirth which cannot die anymore because through the belief in God, through hope of an eternal life, and through the love for the saviour it refreshes itself with divine and abiding sustenance and only achieves its high goal in the hereafter. Belief, hope, and love are the pillars of the Christian church and need for their appreciation no high wisdom, no deep learnedness, but rather pure dispositions, an unspoilt, receptive demeanour and daily self-admonition in order to achieve through practice a degree of solidity of faith which cannot be shaken anymore by any phrases, any scholarly philosophy, or any reproaches. From this small outline you will see how danger-ous it is to want to rattle with self-cleverness its structure which has its foundation in the disposition, which stands on secure pillars and becomes forever more glorious, the more the light of faith achieves dominance in us."

Gomphardt felt seized by the zeal of his friend, the Deacon, and by the deep meaning and animated portrayal of his lecture, and said, "I would have to be unthankful, would have to be without feeling, if your urge to help me did not stir me. Only my feeling of thanks is still no proof of an altered view. I am still sick, I still need the doctor, and in order to show you clearly the malady of my soul, allow me just a few words as reply to your address.

The light of faith guided me for as long as until a shocking episode in life gave my way of thinking and feeling a different direction. As it often happens that you believe something and see yourself afterwards deceived. The doctrine of faith arose in time and can therefore not make us rich for eternity." — "The doctrine of faith", the Deacon interrupted him, "did indeed arise in time, but not religion itself. The latter has its roots in eternity and can and must for this reason, if we once set our eyes on its origin, not be challenged. With the arising of the first humans it was already promised as a basic con-dition of human nature and as salvation from death. But we must not consider the first human incarnation according to the history of the peoples, but rather as epochs of creation in which God called from all that was created the first humans to develop, and taught them to rely on a salvation from death and from sin. In this way the Christian religion ties itself to the story of creation and shows us thereby its connection with God. After the spirit of God propagated itself through the patriarchs and prophets up until the point in time when it was through its divine founder pronounced, prepared and sealed with his death. On this unshakeable foundation rests

Christianity, which teaches us immortality and makes for us the belief in it through the resurrection of the saviour into the indispensable condition."

Gomphardt could not yet entirely understand the meaning of this extensive lecture and asked the Deacon to begrudge him time for sorting it all out in himself. The latter, in the assumption that the former felt at least half overcome, said, "The more precious the plant is which we plan to establish, the more carefully we must go to work. Only when ground and soil are properly prepared can the roots of the introduced plant draw its nourishment into itself. I am pleased with your receptivity and am convinced you will learn to look to heaven with renewed courage and find everything for which noble souls yearn."

The Deacon left and Gomphardt undertook to illuminate the matter in the mirror of his diary that evening.

24th December.

I have gotten to know Christianity from another side without, however, obtaining more truth.

The Christian church is based on the story of the creation and on the history of Israel. According to the usual chronology about three thousand years were needed to lay the foundation, and many centuries to complete the church. It is true no other institution can boast such a result of its conduct. But is the matter therefore more convincing and are the results consequently infallible? Everything stems from God, the grass as much as the human. The former spouts, matures, and withers. The human is born, grows, dies, and decays. Where now is the law of immortality?

Faith should awaken us to life, hope nourish it, and love make us alive for eternity. Anyone who cannot believe has no originator; anyone who does not believe can also not hope, and how it is possible to love if we lack belief and hope? The saviour arose from the dead; will others also rise? Amalie, when you lived, you who believed, hoped, and loved, would you not arise, even if not in the body, then in the soul and grant me certainty about a future life which the senses do not grasp, the understanding does not comprehend, and which all the powers of thought cannot explain? There are no miracles, says the philosophy of the greatest thinkers, and consequently the most important thing which humans believe in is condemned out of hand, to the extent that immortality would be the greatest miracle in that contrary to all laws life would come from death.

Many indeed claim nature confirms this apparent miracle in that from everything which dies before our eyes new beings, new parts of creation arise. It is true. But the new thing is a different thing from that which was previously isolated, existing for itself, and can also not serve in the most distant way as a proof of our personal continuation. Everything continues. Nothing is destroyed but the specific character, the personality flees with the dissolution of the various materials from which we are put together, and death celebrates its triumph with the loss of our ego.

Am I saying this to comfort myself? No, in mourning. With the loss of hope in the hereafter all the threads of my happiness are cut off, and nothing remains for me but the cold resignation to my fate, against which to rebel would be folly in so far as I would also not draw the slightest advantage from it.

The human wishes to live. What does he not wish for? And how little are his wishes fulfilled? Should perhaps, because the less important wishes are so seldom realised, the conclusion be made from it that the highest wish realises itself all the more dependably? The human wishes, the wish drives him to belief, finally to hope, and when faith and hope unite, love comes; thus we see it in all the circumstances of life; and since here the results so rarely correspond to the feelings, no conclusion is to be made, and I stand at the same point at which I stood yesterday."

***

The Deacon, in order to give his student time to think about what he had heard, only returned to visit after five days. With good-natured confidence he addressed Gomphardt as follows.

"I hesitated to visit you in order to not induce you to any overhasty concessions. Views which enclose in themselves our most sacred interests must be examined properly so that, penetrating into our blood, they hold us fast to the path we have set out on. But undaunted, even if you are walking yet with not such a firm step as you perhaps wish! As the youth strengthens himself through expedient activity, the believer does so through more frequently getting inside himself for the strengthening of belief. Allow me a few questions!"

Deacon: "Have you examined the truth of the Christian religion and acknowledged its power?"

Gomphardt: "Deacon! If I must confess to you that I am not in agreement with various points, then I ask you not to take it badly. It is a sort of great unthankfulness to want to not accept things which are proffered amiably as gifts. Only gifts which the donee does not understand how to use are better in the hands of the former owner. I belong to those arrogant men who like to have shown to them what you would like to gift them, but who reserve the right to grasp only for that which pleases them. You will understand me and will not consider my utterances to be an indiscretion or affront."

Deacon: "Can someone straying offend us? Never. Forgive me if I confess openly to you that I consider you to be such a person. You have left the path on which your parents, your relatives, your wife, and everyone who ever had a part in your education and your life course placed you. I, who was present at many of the functions concerning you, who by means of my office and the friendly connection with your house stand in close relation to you, I am obliged to do everything to keep you on the directed life course, and if you become doubtful, to show you the more certain signpost."

Gomphardt: "Are there yet other signposts than those which you have already shown me?"

Deacon: "There are yet others, notwithstanding that those already cited are the most important ones."

Gomphardt: "How can one see the right signpost?"

Deacon: "Through the light of faith."

Gomphardt: "And if such a thing is extinguished?"

Deacon: "You must endeavour to reignite it."

Gomphardt: "How?"

Deacon: "Through inner yearning for it, through prayer, through practice of the Christian virtues which warm our disposition and take it away from that stiff coldness which arises from unbelief."

Gomphardt: "It is such coldness which is creating my misfortune. But I have not caused it. Fate stormed with all the horrors of death into my house and robbed me of the warming radiance of love and of belief."

Deacon: "You have loved and are accordingly capable of loving?"

Gomphardt: "I have loved, am capable of loving. My love was like the precious treasure of a rich man who found his happiness in possession of it. Robbers came, tore from him the treasure, and fortune and joy was gone."

Deacon: "Anyone who places his happiness on a single pillar is already poor in advance. Life offers so many treasures that, if we are not happy, we are ourselves to blame because we do not possess courage and willpower enough to look around properly."

Gomphardt: "Who would not like to renounce poverty and throw themselves in the arms of fortune?"

Deacon: "The headstrong one who has already drafted the plan of happiness and who stipulates to the eternal estate in what way he wants to be happy. The receiver, if he is not entirely blinded, should never stipulate what gifts he considers good to accept. His thing is to accept and to enjoy gratefully. Through that he makes himself worthy of always receiving new gifts and rejoicing every day over a new fortune."

Gomphardt: "In this way, however, the right to ask would be taken from the human."

Deacon: "That no. He should only not wish and ask in reverse — not want to see in spring the richness of autumn, and in autumn the splendour of spring. The human should be reasonable and pious, then he will be blessed with all the good things which are promised to him through the spirit of our sublime religion."

Gomphardt: "I would be unthankful if I did not want to confess to you that such views pass over me without trace, and that I feel especially struck by the last change in your words. Humans would like to possess in summertime winter, in wintertime summer, next to the blessings of autumn the shimmer of spring, the heat of summer, and the snow covered streets of winter. You are right! Truly! Deacon, you are right; but with me autumn is over, and the cold of winter has already turned my heart to ice."

Deacon: "The ice will melt in the sunny beams of belief and of love. A heart like your own cannot close itself off for ever from the higher light which first gives our nature true nobility; hence take heart, the time will come where you will say to me: God is within the human, and he has born witness for me through his son."

Gomphardt asked him to be permitted to think over what had been said, and expressed with an intimacy like never before his thanks for the loving instruction. The Deacon replied, "The eternal truths of our divine religion do not actually need both contemplation and empathising. Great thinkers of our time have dragged the religion down into a book learning and almost destroyed it. Christ must become a feeling, must come alive in us, otherwise he is not in a position to reveal himself and to convince us of the infallibility of his words. The school is incapable here of anything, incapable of anything are the philosophical systems which have followed one another and displaced each other again for a century. The bringing to life of faith is the necessary condition for the task which the ignorant can fulfill just as well as the greatest thinker. Take these few words to heart and do not also then become doubtful when your feelings bristle at first. Only when the soil is loose does the seed penetrate it — only when our hearts are receptive do they take up the doctrine of the apostolic word into themselves."

The Deacon left, and Gomphardt thought for the entire rest of the day about what he had heard.

Before going to bed he sat down at his writing desk before his diary. Before he began writing, he asked himself, "What did I feel and what did I think today?"

30th December.

Feelings and thoughts are the life of humans.

What I heard today penetrated to my heart; but the thoughts find in it a confluence of ideas which seem to be portrayed as a system, but are not one.

Feelings should be the basic truths of religion. In this view admittedly lies such a beneficial generality that you cannot help but wish it were true.

The human can work himself thus into everything which he undertakes so that it seems to live in him. For anyone who endeavours always to believe, this activity and afterwards the belief itself becomes a need. But does the belief become all the more effective as a result? Is immortality, because we have believed in it for years, all the more certain? Have I not believed and hoped my late wife would have had to have reached a happy old age on account of her virtues? What help was this belief, this hope? The principle that the granting must follow the belief stand on such shaky pillars that you cannot possibly support yourself on it. Were the story of Jesus not encroached on from all sides, and almost drawn into the fabulous, words like those I heard today could soothe me; but I must renounce any better outlook, and tolerate my fate with cold surrender.

I will wound the Deacon, who in the calling of his profession and with paternal love seeks to guide me onto a different track, if I oppose for longer. And yet I cannot do anything else, must not feign feelings which I do not have, must not draw what is so sacred to him into the area of my unbelief, provided that I do not want to hurt him. What should I do? To not want to hear him anymore would be hard and unthankful; to hear him and not believe means playing a game with his sacred zeal, a game which would make me despicable to myself. I must leave my estate, leave the place where every space and every tree reminds me of the times of my happiness, is dear to me through the memories. I know no other means. I must leave, even if only for a short time. Perhaps I will find again amongst people foreign to me that which I must not hope for here. Perhaps the change will succeed in defeating my apathy and in showing me life, if not also in more beautiful, then in more various colours.

***

The Departure

The next morning Gomphardt considered once more the decision he had made the day before and read through to this end the appropriate entry of his diary. After he had examined the matter from all sides, saw his incapability here of encouraging and elevating himself in the house of his grief, he made the firm decision to leave this area immediately for a year and to give his feelings a new activity and a different direction amongst people unfamiliar to him.

Three weeks previously a man, equipped with the best references, had turned to him and asked him whether he could be of some assistance to him in his finding employment as administrator of some estate. Gomphardt had promised his assistance without suspecting that he would be in need of such an administrator soon himself. He wrote to this man to give his decision reality straightaway, even in the same hour, and offered him the administration of his own estate. With the return post he received the answer in which the seeker shared his joyous acceptance and at the same time promised to appear himself on the spot in eight days time, to examine the necessary conditions, and, in the case of reaching an agreement, to conclude the contract at once.

When the Deacon visited him again after a few days, he made known to him his decision and gave as motivation for it the disgruntlement of his disposition which was not to be recovered in the place where everything reminded him of his loss. The Deacon, although he had been surprised by this revelation, approved of his intention though and suggested that amongst strangers and far from the place of his grief that elevation of the heart will occur without which no upswing to a higher life view is possible. They spoke about this and that, drafted itinerary after itinerary and parted only when they had travelled in their discussion through all of Germany, a part of Italy, and all the big cities of France.

Gomphardt lived as he had up to now quietly and withdrawn. In his diary he expressed himself over the aim of travelling in general and also in respect to himself, which is passed over here as not belonging in essence to the matter. The appointed administrator came, concluded a contract to Gomphardt's specifications for the period of a year, but on account of a bookkeeping business he had taken over could only start in his position in two months' time. This time also went past without anything special taking place. Even the Deacon refrained from his business of conversion, in the safe certainty Gomphardt would, when the wounds of his heart were healed by the various impressions of the world, come to a better conviction and would find again that balance which is only to be produced by the uniting of the here and now with the hereafter.

After two months the administrator arrived, and Gomphardt made preparations for the journey. He gathered once more all his servants and workers about himself, thanked them for their devotion to him and his late wife, and recommended them to the administrator as their superior who would from now on administer the estate in his name.

Everybody was stirred and asked him to return again soon. The Deacon, who was also present, answered in the name of everyone and said, "Mr Gomphardt, you have always treated your servants like a father does his children. This everybody recognises and entreats heaven for your blessings and health. Everyone will remain obedient with love and loyalty and take care of your property under the leadership of the new administrator with the same punctuality as under the eyes of their master. This I promise in everyone's name and ask God that he might guide your steps."

Gomphardt had arranged a small celebration for those present and had food, wine, and beer carried out so that all could enjoy themselves on it. He was invited by the Deacon as guest to lunch the following day in order to speak with him once more about his disposition and about his views on life absolutely undisturbed.

The day passed for his people amidst joyfulness, jokes, and song. When they made preparations to break off, an old servant grasped his glass and said aloud, as he bared his head, "To the memory of the too soon departed wife of our master!" Everybody drank quietly, and most of them crept away with tears in their eyes.

Bernhard, a servant whom Gomphardt had brought with himself from the university to the estate and had also decided to take on the journey, informed him of this. Gomphardt felt surprised and moved in a melancholic way; nevertheless it did his heart well though to find such unfeigned sympathy amongst his own. "The people are good," he said, "when they obey their feelings; but as soon as they ponder and calculate, they stray from the path of natural good-naturedness and of happiness, and wander, instead of into a rose garden, into a rough field which indeed also nourishes after a fashion, but brings no enjoyment and no pleasure."

Hardly had twelve o'clock struck the next day than Gomphardt entered the Deacon's house to take his midday meal there. The Deacon had made arrangements to host him, even if not nobly, well enough. But hardly had they finished eating than the discussion got serious, and the Deacon called on everything to portray to his parting friend once more all the points of light of the Christian religion and to explain the benefits of it. Gomphardt often seemed carried away by his teaching and thanked him when it was time to leave with such warmth that you would have thought he was convinced by the truth of it perfectly. Only his mind was much too far from such apostolic views for it to have been possible for feelings to win over the ingrained doubts. Irrespective of his thanks being no less feigned, to the contrary, he said with complete conviction and sacred earnest that if he had been shown in his earlier years the spirit of the Christian religion in such a way, he would not now have need of travelling out into the world to learn to believe again.

The Deacon at this confession placed his hand on the shoulder of his friend and said, "Even the wish to be able to believe reveals the power of creation of eternal life in itself.

Hence be brave! We go our different ways, you driven by the wish, I by the belief, and truly, by means of these two powers we are connected in the most intimate way and will see each other again in the hereafter where belief and wish raise themselves to view."

Gomphardt made arrangements to leave and asked the Deacon whether he did not have for him still a wish or a task for thinking about on the way. The Deacon replied, "I would probably know something I would like to give you to think about, if I did not fear making myself guilty of too great a presumption."

Gomphardt: "You misjudge me if you fear such a thing. Do I not know that you want my happiness, and that you are saddened only to not see me as happy as you wish?"

Deacon: "Are you ready to confirm with your word what I will ask of you? Assuming that you yourself regard my desire as acceptable?"

Gomphardt: "Even without this prerequisite I would have given you my word."

Deacon: "Well, then promise me never to mock religious views and pious beliefs."

Gomphardt: "I promise that."

Deacon: "Never intentionally flee the opportunity by which you could obtain again your earlier beliefs in God and in immortality."

Gomphardt: "I promise that."

Deacon: "You are in full adulthood and in strong health. In these years sensuality often exercises a greater force than in the time of youth. Promise me to control yourself always and never forget your dignity as human and as man of honour."

Gomphardt: "I promise that."

Deacon: "I have yet one more request, only I fear almost to express it because it could appear as if I wanted to limit your free will."

Gomphardt: "To subject oneself to a limitation in the interest of a friend is duty. I give my word in advance."

Deacon: "Then listen. The request is odd; only it is based on years of experience ... Never enter into the society of the freemasons!"

Gomphardt: "Your wish is my law. I promise never to enter into that association without your agreement."

Deacon: "I am gladdened by your word and am reassuring myself with the thought that you will through your assent preserve yourself from further deviations and be connected forever with me. God guide you on your way and lead you healthy and happy back home to us."

Gomphardt felt deeply moved at this parting. He offered the Deacon his hand, spoke a few more words of emotional thanks and departed.

Arriving home, he thought over the events of the past two days and could not prevent himself saying, "The human can be happy if he is capable of opening his heart to all who are around him and of feeling their sympathy."

He rang for his servant, with his help making everything ready for being able to depart the next day at the earliest time. Before he went to bed that night, he sat down at his writing desk in order to express himself frankly now again in his diary in the accustomed place.

3rd March.

I am leaving you, you friendly place where I so often expressed my feelings and thoughts in solitary silence. Even now I want to talk and confess how I am feeling as I take my leave of here.

Humans are good, all of them, when they stand without prejudice towards one another.

I felt abandoned and was for a long time not as much as I imagined. Amalie left me. Nature commanded her to part. If I were to have the belief in seeing her again, I could be, even if not entirely, somewhat happy though.

Love is the bond of souls. I felt yesterday and today how easily the heart opens to its light and, warmed by it, beats in pure bliss.

Why are humans often so cold, why do they withdraw themselves from the heaven which resides within them? Death is a monster, but there is a still greater one, passion. Its furies have indeed spared me up to now, but wherever I looked, these monsters were raging and making humans who were destined for happiness unhappy.

Why does this general observation only occur to me now? Is it perhaps a premonition of my future in which I will wander amongst strangers who will entwine me with greed, ambition, obstinacy, and thousands of temptations, and will poison my heart?

Of what am I afraid then? Of humans? No, of the forms which I do not understand, and to which I will be able to connect myself with effort.

Why did my belief have to have been torn away from me? With it I did not need to go out into the world and would have possessed everything for reaching the destination of my existence.

World! You stand open to me, in you I can look around. But beyond you there is no destination, on the other side it is dark, and the more I endeavour to see light, all the more I see only my incapability.

If I could believe, as the Deacon wishes, could take from the principle — that belief brings to life — only a glimmer of natural necessity, I would hold myself with ardent soul to it and seek my happiness in the hereafter.

Whoever then knows that there comes a better day bears the troubles of the moment with courage. But to those who have no outlook, no beliefs, to them the present is an almost unbearable burden.

The future is secretive, the present reigns. What it gives us is reality, and could gift us satisfaction if the dark outlook of the future did not make every enjoyment unpalatable.

I must go out into the world. Here, I feel, I am going under. I must get to know people who think and feel like I do, in order with their eyes to test the truth or inadequacy of my assertions and to reinforce myself in them.

Miserable solace! You will enjoy yourself, but sensually; you will not see the future in the frenzy of the moment, will not want to see it and will be happy in this way through self-deception.

Truth is happiness, say the wise ones of all times; consequently those who seek it in self-deception have cheated themselves of happiness and truth.

Labyrinthine it lies before me, and no exit shows itself to the eyes that seek. I am going into the world, into the great labyrinth; perhaps I will find there a sign showing the way out of the confused corridors.

Amalie, I am going! If you still live, I am not going away. To me it is as if you were standing here wishing me luck on my journey. To me it is as if everything lived around me to say farewell to me. What sort of feeling is that which knows how to animate everything? Is it that belief? No, it is love, is the dependency on everything which we make use of, it is the sacred might of custom which gives to the lifeless things language and meaning. Farewell, my room, farewell, my house! Farewell your fields and meadows, to all, farewell to all which captivates my heart, refreshes my soul, and saw me happy by Amalie's side.

***

Seized by melancholy, he closed the book, placing it in his satchel in order to have it at hand on the journey as often as he wanted to make use of it.

The next morning, straight after five o'clock, he departed from his house for the next post station with a few horses. All his people had positioned themselves by the way in order to yet say their farewells to him. This attentiveness made the most beneficial impression on him, so that he left his estate in the most benevolent state of mind and promised to himself to retain the feeling of pure humanity under all circumstances.

***

Part 2: Freemasonry in Social Respect

Beautiful it is to live in joy in the circle of humans;
But the spectre of death scares off the joy.

Indifferentism

Gomphardt's first destination was Hm., where he arrived on the third day in good time, stopped at the tavern R., and was directed to three rooms, two for himself and one for his servant. He was, since he dispatched the postilion with a good tip and indicated with his arrangements that he'd be making a long stay, received with an attentiveness which almost embarrassed him. "I must now accustom myself to everything," he said to himself when he was alone, called his servant, unpacked his things, and arranged himself in a way that he did not lack much in comparison to his rooms at home.

He had in Hm., partly from the university, partly through addresses given to him, but partly also through business connections in which he had been drawn by his significant possessions, many claims on persons and families whom he resolved to visit in order to obtain in this way an entry into the world at large. To this end he rented his own hired coach and a hired servant, and drove directly the next day to several families. The reception was obliging and warm everywhere so that he soon felt at home. Before three weeks had passed, he saw himself introduced to all the clubs and gatherings. These gatherings, regardless of each putting forward a different tendency, all agreed in enjoying life and ignoring the unpleasant things in it. It was understood of itself that with such gatherings, where fleeting goals prevailed under meaningful pretences, a well laid table must never be lacking, which was seen from all sides as the cornerstone of true living.

With these gatherings Gomphardt had the opportunity to get to know a few men of his age who alongside the social life devoted themselves to the arts and in part to the sciences too, and everywhere that aimed at promoting or to protecting such things they placed themselves at the forefront. Among them was found a Mr Riccort, who drew our traveller to himself through uninhibited conduct, an educated mind, and obliging goodwill. He was often seen visiting this man. Riccort also spoke frequently with him, and every time their conversation turned, after the usual news of the day had been discussed, to the positive goals of humanity and the means for fulfilling them. Riccort seemed in such discussions often to have a question on the tip of his tongue, but without expressing it. Gomphardt noticed that and asked what the cause was. Riccort responded, "Sometimes when I hear you speak, I believe I am certain in a presumption which I felt straightaway at our first meeting; when I put you to another test, however, I again become doubtful. Hence I will ask with plain words: are you a freemason?"

Gomphardt: "No."

Riccort: "What, not a freemason? Then I will propose you today. You will hopefully permit it?"

Gomphardt: "I regret I must say no again."

Riccort: "What, travelling around the world without being a freemason? That is just as if a journeyman craftsman wanted to travel without the book to record his jobs and hours. The educated of all peoples have drawn a circle around the earth in which they only allow entry to those who belong to them."

Gomphardt: "I am here without being a freemason, have been taken in with hospitality and warmth."

Riccort: "That may well be, but some remain unknown to you, some circles closed off. Freemasonry first gives us true entry into the life; for it excludes by statute, meanwhile all society opens itself to it. You must become a freemason, not for the sake of others, but for your own sake."

Gomphardt: "Friend, I cannot; but do not believe that childish obstinacy or prejudices are holding me back, no, I gave a fatherly friend my word never to enter into that society."

Riccort: "How can one just give his word to such a thing!"

Gomphardt: "As you give it sometimes without making much of it in the moment. But the obligation to keep one's word is not lifted by changed views."

Riccort: "You are right, although you can also in such cases be to severe with yourself. Only that is a matter of each to their own. Here it is to be asked, is the word not to be returned by your friend?"

Gomphardt: "With difficulty. Especially with the principles which I see developed here amongst the members of the institution, it would not be permitted to happen."

Riccort: "The principles are not bad though?"

Gomphardt: "Not bad, but yet not of the sort to move my friend thereby to release me from my word."

Riccort: "Eh, I see! You criticise in the end our principles; there I must make a stand."

Gomphardt: "Good, make a stand and tell me what freemasonry is, what it does, what things it discusses, and if this appears convincing enough to me, then I will write to my friend and ask him for the release from my word."

Riccort: "You would like to know what freemasonry is, what it does, and what matters it discusses. As only a rational man is yet able to ask! Freemasonry wants to live rationally and dispenses with all the nonsense to which prejudices, superstition, fanaticism, blind faith, and even learnedness lead so easily with humans."

Gomphardt: "That is saying a lot; in essence, however, so little that you still do not know what freemasonry is. If I questioned you about each of your expressions individually, I am certain you would end up embarrassed to answer me succinctly."

Riccort: "I ending up embarrassed opposite someone who is uninitiated? Watch! So ask, if you feel like it! But now now, another time. I must prepare my shield and lance first in order to attend to you in this battle as is proper. You shall see that I do not wear the apron in vain, you uninitiated swordsman, you! I will go, but will come again tomorrow to eat lunch with you, and after the meal the battle shall commence. Until we meet again!"

Gomphardt: "Until we meet again then! Only sharpen your lance, that is, your tongue well; for I have already seen that I will not be defeated so easily."

Riccort arrived once more at Gomphardt's to fetch him for a gathering of freemasons. "It is indeed not usual", he said, "to lead uninitiated people into our little meetings, only I have given my friends hope you will, provided you enjoy it with us, be taken in as a freemason, and they found no objection to that. You see how certain I am of my affair," he continued, "in that I give you the opportunity to examine the terrain before our battle." Gomphardt had indeed for that evening had his ticket for the play obtained already; for his friend's sake he had given it though to his servant and went to the freemasons' gathering.

He had never before thought seriously about freemasonry and was girding himself on the way for the thousands of things which he would hear, and was therefore very astonish-ed when he saw the company distinguished from any other dining or drinking club by nothing but that you moved more at ease and expressed yourself frankly about all topics which were brought up, both in praise and rebuke.

"How did you like it in our little circle?", Riccort asked when they were on their way home together. "Tomorrow," Gomphardt replied, "I will give you my answer on the field of battle." They wished each other a good night, and each went to his own residence.

Riccort appeared punctually the next day and dined with Gomphardt at the table d'hôte at which several members of the previous evening's company had gathered. They sat in the vicinity of Riccort and Gomphardt and already looked on the latter as half one of their own. After the meal they took their leave with the promise of seeing each other soon, but the two adversaries took themselves up to Gomphardt's room to test their strength against each other. Riccort began immediately, "We are at the battlefield. I am the one challenged, thus the attack is owed to me." — "You see me in a state of defence", Gomphardt responded, "and will not achieve the victory so easily." — "Well now," the former said, "listen to me and give me an answer to my questions. I well belong to those who with everything they undertake make such an important demeanour, as if it were about the welfare or woe of an entire land. Meanwhile, when it is about assisting a friend or my relative, I apprehend my man. I say this first so that it does not surprise you too much if I make use of the tone of a mentor with you. I ask you therefore, what do you understand by the term humanity?"

Gomphardt: "All humans who have lived, are living, and will yet live."

Riccort: "Have all who were, are, and will be then one and the same life's goal?"

Gomphardt: "I cannot think of it being any other way."

Riccort: "And you believe everyone strives towards one and the same goal?"

Gomphardt: "No less."

Riccort: "To that truly belongs a great metaphysical power for bringing the most diverse ideas, plans, businesses, stages of development, classes, and dispositions under one law."

Gomphardt: "The eternity which absorbs all who exist could easily also govern all according to a law."

Riccort: "Eternity! Indeed! But will it, can it do it? Who will worry about things which lie so far outside our field of view that we are not in a position to have even only the slight- est idea of them?"

Gomphardt: "And nonetheless your associations, indeed under other names, aim again at something higher. Morality, humanity, and human welfare are the keywords of your meetings. Give me information on how your fleeting conduct is to be reconciled with such serious life views."

Riccort: "Three kingdoms lie in a triangle next to each other. Two of them get into diplomatic disputes, and when the pen no longer suffices, one grasps for the sword. Now the question arises: with which of the two shall the third king, who has been calm up to now, support? — The latter answers: I shall remain neutral and will at the conclusion of the war support the one from whom I draw the most advantage. This little story is not from me, but rather taken from an old chronicle, according to which a true patriot brought his bellicose fatherland's attention to its position."

Gomphardt: "I cannot find the application to our case."

Riccort: "And yet it lies so close to it. The two warring kingdoms are our spirit and our senses. We stand by with our personality, our ego, and remain neutral."

Gomphardt: "In what does such neutrality consist?"

Riccort: "We give to the spirit what is of the spirit, and to the senses what is of the senses. In this way we produce a balance which is fitting to our nature and provides us with all the pleasures of the senses and of the spirit."

Gomphardt: "It is wonderful how you can give the most heterogeneous views an appearance of truth and of strong principles."

Riccort: "There is nothing wonderful here, but instead the absolute law of nature. Who surely would sacrifice all enjoyments to the fear of immortality and a judge for eternity, as long as he is still uncertain of immortality and an eternal judge? Would that not be foolishness, indeed directly contrary to the course of nature which has not put us in such a beneficent uncertainty in vain? Because we are not certain whom we belong to, are not certain who the mightiest is, we remain neutral and fulfil thereby the law of a positive necessity."

Gomphardt: "This neutrality is the most terrible indifferentism* which is to be thought of."

Riccort: "Indifferentism or neutrality, it is all the same. So as not to work for one party alone, we endorse from indifferentism none. So as to not have to fight, we remain neutral. It all leads to the one thing. A fool, however, is someone who ruins his time with brooding and does not endorse us, the true students of wisdom."

Gomphardt: "And freemasonry teaches and spreads this spirit?"

Riccort: "None other. Indeed not so clearly and drily as I expressed myself now. But everybody has a presentiment of the matter themselves and is led by instinct to the practice of this doctrine which is only shared in symbols. And truly, all declare themselves to be very well, so long as this double relationship exists. Only when we turn ourselves entirely to

---

* [Tr.: indifferentism is the belief that differences in religious belief are of no importance.]

this or that side does the joy leave us, in that sensual pleasures without spirit lead to over-satiation, but spiritual pleasures, removed from the senses, lead to a dryness which obstructs the access to any purely human feeling."

Gomphardt: "Irregardless that I agree in essence with your views, I cannot agree though to pay homage to a philosophy according to which the human only possesses in a base, neutral state an appearance of independence. According to what has been said, the human is condemned to an immoral passivity which grants him nothing but to watch idly whilst all around him is activity. I have resolved to seek the truth, on whichever side I find it, I would be ashamed not to agree with one or the other part only so as to see who will carry the victory from it. I do not believe in immortality, but not from the delights of the senses, but rather because nature tells us the dead cannot live. Humanity has notwithstanding this its own inner joys which belong to the heart, the soul, and the spirit, and have more reality than the opulence of the meal and the titillation of satisfied sensual enjoyments. We love humans, they us, and in this reciprocation lies a magic which is of paradisical origin, and which for perfect happiness lacks nothing but eternity. Only this eternity cannot be grasped and gained by those born from dust, and hence its unreachability is not a real evil, but rather only an imagined evil, which is approximately like the misfortune of the millionaire who worries himself to death because he is not four million rich."

Riccort laughed aloud at this last comparison, and responded, "You speak like a book, you make an effort like a pedagogue to prove me wrong, whilst you express my views, only even better than me. What do I desire different then than that we should not worry ourselves over what we do not possess, perhaps will never possess. The four million must not trouble us; but if it arrives, then we will strive to use it properly. If a fortune smiles on us one day in the hereafter unexpectedly, then it should find us capable of enjoying it; but for us to dispense with it for the sake of joys in the here and now would be absurdity and absolutely not to be excused before the court of nature and reason. See! That is the Aristotelian golden mean, is wisdom, freemasonry, and the philosophy of every free, thinking human."

Gomphardt: "Your tongue is as seductive as the sirens' song. When you speak in such a way —"

Riccort: "Have no worries! — Regardless of almost everyone living according to my principles, they seldom though have the courage to hear such or to confess to it. It is enough that my theory is practised without knowing and wanting to and is thereby factually confirmed."

Gomphardt would certainly have wished to be able to refute the claims of his friend; but since he at base was of the same view, remaining even on the point of immortality still behind him, he remained silent and made the suggestion to continue the discussion another time, walk in the open air now and refresh themselves following such a philosophical conversation.

Riccort accepted the suggestion, and both spent the day amidst diversions of various sorts.

In the evening Gomphardt sat down to his diary and said to himself, before he began writing, "I must express myself, tell myself so that I do not, blinded by strange ideas, become apathetic to positive truths."

5th June.

The great world is different than I thought.

What would my fatherly friend, the Deacon, say if he had to hear conversations like the one I had today? He would feel sorry for me and my conversation partner. What would Riccort have said if he ever had to hear me speaking with the Deacon? He would have felt called to likewise feel sorry for us.

Immortality is the great question. Some believe in it and are happy. As the parents, the teacher, and the pastor have taught them, they believe thus and rejoice in the future like the present. To be able to believe is a great fortune. Even if the belief is not fulfilled, it has though sweetened the life. I praise the one who expressed it that belief leads to life; he has given humanity more than all the world improvers of ancient and modern times, than all the wise and great men of world history. Belief is the support of the aged, is the solace of the oppressed. The shackled slave gazes up through faith to heaven for help and sees there his freedom. The wailing mother sees her child in the coffin and hopes through the grave and coffin for a happy reunion. Where is there a misfortune which belief does not lessen, where a sorrow whose tears it cannot dry? The belief in immortality is the highest good which the human can possess. I, the unbeliever, invoke this truth.

Why must I know this good and not also possess it? This question contains the puzzle of my life, which I still have no prospect of solving.

***

The Historian

Riccort had not yet given up on the idea of bringing Gomphardt so far as to have himself submitted to the freemasons, and united to this end with another who treated the matter with more seriousness not only from the cosmopolitan neutral, but also from the purely historical point of view. This man had already frequently been in Gomphardt's company, had taken pleasure in his natural openness and in his many-sided knowledge, and undertook with pleasure the guiding of a worthy member into the institution. He and Riccort came to an agreement to invite Gomphardt alone to his place and to sit with him, if he then warmed to it, for as long as until he were to have given his assent to them.

It was not Riccort's thing to put an intention off for long; hence he invited both those involved to his place the next day and made arrangements that they could not be disturbed by anyone.

Gomphardt had noticed soon enough that the small company had assembled only for his sake, and said, "Here all eyes are on me. All the same! Amongst friends you can put up with anything. Even if they challenge us to battle, it happens only to strengthen our powers through practice so that we, if it ever gets serious, are properly prepared." Riccort replied, "Admittedly all eyes are on you and indeed so seriously that we are resolved to call up everything to bring it about that you connect with us in the closest way and enter our circle of brothers. But now it is not yet time to speak about it; when you have strengthened yourself a little, the good thoughts will come by themselves."

They sat down at a small but well laid table. All three had a good taste of it. Gomphardt made the remark in his feeling of comfort that sound appetite and good food were such positive pleasures that no stoic and no eremite could belittle them by mere conceit. "Only it's a pity", he continued, "that the joys are so seldom and not for the common good of all humanity." Riccort replied, "You are sentimentality personified and born to be a freemason. We need such a treasure of the soul who fills himself up everywhere and finds opportunity everywhere to give. We are too happy, too easygoing, too good, I would like to say, and often forget from sheer fulfilment of our obligations the main obligation of sharing the feelings of others and making them as it were our own."

Gomphardt, who had just grasped his glass to drink from, placed it back on the table and said, turned to Riccort, "You often express in your wantonness things which would have to surprise anyone. To share the feelings of others and make them as it were your own is the main activity of human life. Someone who cannot do that is not yet human, but rather a block which, to speak with the Bible, is lacking the animating breath." — "So it is," Riccort said, "anyone who closes their heart, does not occasionally bear it openly and also in their face is a hypochondriac, an enemy of humanity, and should for the good of others have himself measured the sooner the better for the coffin as his Sunday best."

The third member of the company, Mr Rinkam, a scholar who, in possession of a sufficient means, dedicated himself mainly to the sciences, had, with the exception of a few of the usual polite words, not yet taken part in the conversation, and considered the current mood to be suited for beginning his intent and, as per his promise, drawing the proselyte into the net. He took up the conversation and said, "You will pardon my frankness if I direct a few words to you. You are displaying in your words and convictions a degree of humanity that you could be taken for a freemason of the first class. For this reason our friend Riccort has called on you to allow yourself to be proposed by us. Only according to his information you find nothing in this society which you do not already possess to an elevated degree; hence I have taken it upon myself to show you freemasonry from its essential and serious point of view. If you will just give me a few moments of your attention, you will easily see the truth and the importance of my portrayal.

From time immemorial the best and most educated of the human race have sought to unite in order to establish as much good as possible and to remove the evil. Such an undertaking often infringed on those in power, on the prejudices of the crowd, on the arrogance of wealth, and hence it was seen necessary to conceal themselves and to execute the plan in silence. This secretiveness led, however, again to other evils which had not previously been suspected; the societies expanded and frequently hid the direction of their work even amongst themselves. This gave cause for splits, confusions, and struggles so that you often had to fear that the entire institution would go under. But thanks be to the giver of all light, the true freemasonry emerged victorious from all the storms.

For a long time there was uncertainty over the means of controlling the uprooted malady. A few suggested scientific education, others strict morality, a third group cleaning from the Christian religion of all human statutes, a fourth even a sort of religion of reason. But none of these suggestions could suffice, since, if the temple of freemasonry should encompass all of humanity, you could not make everyone into scholars, and morality is something very relative in that in another place and at another time it changes itself; then furthermore not all humans possess the mind for a purified religion; and finally a faith of reason already contains a contradiction in itself. Finally a few eager, knowledgeable members thought of history and found through it the light for separating the true from the false and for reestablishing the order in its original purity."

"Through history?", Gomphardt inserted in astonishment.

"No less," Rinkam continued. "When a tree sprouts too many water shoots and they are not immediately removed, then they grow almost unbelievably, taking the sustenance from the real branches so that you obtain instead of fruit only leaves and ever new false branches. Such a tree cannot be reestablished in any other way than if you learn to distinguish exactly the bad branches from the good, cut away the former and thereby supply the natural sustenance to the others. Thus it happened here — through knowledge of the bad you got to know the good, and thus we work, free from all harmful growths, on the glorious trunk of our institution and may deliver it confidently to our children, grandchildren, and later progeny."

Gomphardt had listened attentively to this talk and said, "Thank you for the information which you have provided me on an in any case important matter." — "Now, and your judgement?", Riccort asked, interrupting him. "I cannot say now," replied Gomphardt. "Mr Rinkam has given me his explanations with such amiable and open-hearted goodness that I would find it very unneighbourly to not thank him approvingly. He has shared his views with me; another time I will betray mine. But for now I remain silent in order not to irritate a man of integrity by opposition."

Riccort: "Here no irritation can take place. We are resolved to make you one of us, and hence you must answer whether you are pleased with our affair or not."

Gomphardt: "Speaking sincerely, I cannot find fault with it. Were I free, I would join with you, but not on account of the matter, but rather the persons who carry it on, whose light and yet noble sense pleases me. Mr Rinkam's deep insights have not just today awakened my respect. But the matter does not have value for me in my place and mood to see me caused to ask my friend for the release from my word."

Riccort: "What don't you like about the matter?"

Gomphardt: "That it is no matter from all that I have heard up to now."

Riccort: "Would it be no matter to learn to walk between darkness and light in beneficial shadow?"

Gomphardt: "The winegrower does not shy from the rays of the sun in order to extract good wine."

Riccort: "Would it be no matter to choose the best from a number of bad things?"

Gomphardt: "Precisely this way of going about things makes me suspicious of the matter."

Riccort: "How so?"

Gomphardt: "I had an acquaintance who, so as to learn to judge character, went daily into the madhouse."

Riccort: "Well, and the result?"

Gomphardt: "Was that in a period of three years he had to be taken himself into the madhouse."

Riccort: "No, that is too awful. — Rinkam, brother! Defend yourself and do not let such shame lie on us."

Rinkam: "His analogy is terrible. But who can judge whether something true, even if applied to us, does not lie in it?"

He offered his hand to Gomphardt and said, "You are a free man; do not let yourself be bribed by shimmering apologies. Accept the assurance of my respect and friendship, and if you consider me worthy of the same, then I ask you for your own."

Gomphardt replied to this address with the usual innocence, and all three abandoned themselves undisturbed to the feeling of their mutual goodwill and spoke about various topics which more or less concerned the fate and circumstances of human life, but did not touch closely on freemasonry. At the close the talk returned again to that, and Riccort reproached Rinkam for having done so little for the intended plan of winning Gomphardt over to the order. "I have done what I could," Rinkam replied. "His analogy surprised me a lot. Only I am not giving up hope, he will yet decide when I say to him our temple is not yet extended. Or, in order to remain with the tree per the earlier analogy, the saying applies: by their fruits you shall recognise them*. Who can say whether the fruits which we foster openly are already the most perfect and sprung from the real branches? None of us all, as I know it, is in the position to. We are still in the process of searching, of purifying, and for that we need effective workers, and it is there I believe that our friend Gomphardt would fulfill a high duty if he decided to join with us and help to seek with his open and uncorrupted mind for the crown of this tree."

Gomphardt became contemplative over this last turn, and said finally, "Where it now concerns our duties, there is no

---

*   [Tr.: cf. Matthew 7:16.]

decision to make, because we are then forced. But one more question I will yet allow myself. Which is the real fruit of the tree? By what do you recognise it? And what consequences arise from it for humanity?" Rinkam replied, "Over that I must remain silent, not because I must not or would not like to speak, but rather because I do not know anything to say about it. As much though I must say, there is far more contained in freemasonry than we know so far. Formerly the matter was well-known, now it seems to have been lost and can only be found again through zealous research. This for our friend Gomphardt. If he ever feels urged, he will come himself to us; now he should follow the path of his heart."

After that midnight was not far off anymore and after, on the inducement of Riccort, they had arranged to meet in a similar way once more like today at Gomphardt's, the three friends parted and each for themselves thought over at home the fruits of the day. Gomphardt sat down, as late as it was even, to his diary, from which we extract the following.

7th June.

History should teach! Can it do that? It delivers examples, but no theory. I have studied the histories of the greatest heroes of ancient and modern times without thereby having become a hero or having learned the art of commanding only a small corps, much less an army. What use it to us to know that Ptolemy, Euclid, and others have calculated if we do not learn to calculate ourselves? Were freemasonry an essential matter, then it could be named, as history it remains only a single branch of world history and would have to, if it were of high importance, have been brought to general knowledge long ago by the historians who pay attention to all the branches of human ability and knowledge.

Rinkam would almost have taken me by surprise. His sincerity and his feeling of obligation possess a power that will conquer those who are not on their guard. My freedom to think has led me into the night of unbelief; it shall yet provide me with light if ever any is to be obtained.

The Historian

***

The Propaganda

The day on which Riccort and Rinkam had promised to come to Gomphardt's was tending towards its end when they arrived at his place with a third friend. When the latter was introduced under the name of Reinthal, Gomphardt responded smiling, "It seems my friends have enlisted reserves. I must put up with it, and if I cannot stand firm, can surrender to discretion." The new guest replied, "The battle for friendship and fraternal love is always of use, even if we are struck down." — "So too do I think," Gomphardt responded and asked those present to take a seat.

It would be going too far to repeat everything which was spoken on this evening about philosophy and freemasonry; only a conversation of Reinthal and Gomphardt's, whereby the others remained silent, must be cited here on account of the matter. The talk returned to the importance of history and the claim that freemasonry through it alone could obtain its true standpoint and the light which it had to seek and to spread. Gomphardt disputed this and the following conversation unwound.

Reinthal: "If humanity did not have any history what would it be?"

Gomphardt: "What it is now, a species of thinking beings gifted with free willpower."

Reinthal: "What, and you believe humanity would without history be at the same point of perfection as now?"

Gomphardt: "I believe that humanity without history would not have many things which it possesses, but that it would give judgement over many things much more freely and more intelligently."

Reinthal: "That goes against nature, which brings everything by and by to maturity."

Gomphardt: "If you only see humanity as a great tree, then I must concede to you. But if it is a forest and every individual is a tree, then, like we see it in trees, the perfection of the whole lies in every individual."

Reinthal: "The idea is new, but contradicts experience."

Gomphardt: "Not at all. History is good, delivers us many examples by which we strive to measure ourselves, to be equal to it, but even history shows us too that directly where one works without its influence the most excellent geniuses come into being. The Greek artists had no art history, had to draw from within themselves and delivered masterworks which have not been reached, much less surpassed. Xenophon, Plato, Socrates, Parrhasius, Apelles, the father of poetry, Homer, had no sources but free human nature which develops according to its own inherent laws and which places everyone who is in a position to observe its activity in the right standpoint."

Reinthal: "According to this view humanity would lose the possibility of progress, and nobody would have the power to leave the point on which nature had randomly placed them, much less to exceed it. It is the most sublime idea which philosophy can give us to see humanity as a great unity which has its youth, its adolescence, and its adulthood and after this its maturity, and to conclude from that its ever ascending state of culture and constantly growing civilisation. I would like to say that anyone who cannot work up enthusiasm for such thought has not yet received any initiation or any baptism and wanders amongst humanity as a heathen."

Gomphardt: "The idea of a continuous growth and progress of human nature is as an idea the most sublime thing which human fantasy has been able to dream up and which the understanding can imagine; the matter itself, however, is a far greater dogma than the ether-winged Adam of the Theosophers and Pietists. No species of all the products of nature delivers the slightest proof of the possibility for such a propaganda. The human alone wants in proud arrogance to know that his species, originating as a sort of animal, is developing into a seeming divinity."

Reinthal: "The human is amongst all products capable of an uninterrupted perfection and increased development, whereas the other creatures and plants are bound to the characteristics of their specific roots."

Gomphardt: "The first human was exactly as perfect as the last will be. Where the human finds himself, where place and circumstances draw him, there he unfolds the highest possible perfection his species is entitled to. If the first humans did not have the school wisdom and training of our time, they possessed instead an almost infallible, rational instinct which compensated them for all our knowledge. Craftsmanship, cunning, cleverness, willpower, magnanimity, bravery, practical knowledge of nature and of the living spirit which flows through it, were according to all historical information a peculiarity of any primitive people through which they wound as well through the unpleasant circumstances of life as we do with our learnedness. The wife of a farmer in the deepest forest who has not left its narrow bounds during her life rules her household in her way as certainly and as orderly as the educated townswoman does her own. The raftsman knows the weather of the coming week from the stars. Everywhere there is perfection, everywhere maturity; the entire difference consists in the detail to which you devote yourself. By aptitude, certain gradations excepted, all humans are equal from the first to the last and this is true for all who reside on earth."

Reinthal: "This limitation is unworthy of humanity, is spiritually deadening and draws the human down into the class of animals."

Gomphardt: "That may well be, but the matter is no less true as a result."

Reinthal: "No other creature is capable of such a culture and development as the human."

Gomphardt: "The human is capable of a human development, the animal of an animal development; both, however, remain through the development always true to their species. The horse, raised in the stable, is milder and more docile than that in a free state. The former possesses through training a number of characteristics which the other does not have — it knows its master, its name, recognises from the sign hung from the house where you can provide it with feed, in short a number of things which often astound us. Now it is to be asked, is it therefore a more perfect horse than that which has never seen a stable and not felt any whip? For the human it is in every way more useful, in terms of its essence, however, it has won nothing; to the contrary, if it were about rescuing itself from danger, fighting with enemies, or seeking fodder in unfavourable weather, then the so-called wild or free horse would far surpass the most trained one. I did not want thereby to say it would be better to renounce culture, but I wanted to show that in culture there does not reside any positive progress, but rather only a seeming progress. This truth can be reinforced by examples from all the kingdoms of nature, and I must say that those who doubt it do not have the courage to look nature in the eye, and console themselves in their weakness with the growth of the whole."

Reinthal: "But how does it stand according to your views with the eternal justness of the creator which we must assume though under all circumstances?"

Gomphardt: "I ask where such a justness is if we assume our forefathers to be dependent children, us to be youths, and only our descendants after several thousand years to be men and in the state of maturity? If we then look further past the prime of man and see a senility in which humanity sinks down again to weakness and finally death?"

Reinthal: "Humanity cannot die anymore; it will continue to grow and cultivate itself always."

Gomphardt: "And how far or how high does it climb in the end? Perhaps until it itself becomes God or at least to an ether-winged species, where it penetrates to the centre of the earth and then again circles around the world system in the flight of thought? Anyone who places the beginning too high goes astray. Anyone who assumes an eternity of growth is deceiving themselves twice over, because you do not find there any stopping anymore when a rational standstill is demanded. This is the outlook if we see history as a doctrine which should serve as the guide to climbing ever higher. We must find the truth within ourselves, all other paths lead to errors whose entire worth consists in being able to quarrel over them."

Riccort, for whom this conversation had become too serious, now entered it and said, "Gomphardt, you are not to be bettered, and if we finally give up on you, then you have to ascribe it to your own obstinacy."

Gomphardt: "You will not give up on me, and our other two friends won't either. No man of honour can take offence if I speak how I think and feel. I have devoted myself to the truth, unconcerned over whether it shows itself in friendly or unfriendly form. Only I must say as much, that I prefer your neutrality above all that I have heard."

Riccort: "Much honour for me."

Gomphardt: "But you too I will never join. I consider it unmanly to diligently watch two disputing parties only for the sake of advantage and not have the courage to assist that on whose side right is. Hence I ask my dear friends to accept the assurance from me that I would feel honoured through your efforts to be introduced into your society, but at present can make no use of your kindness."

"Obstinacy, nothing but obstinacy!", Riccort cried out. "But you desire it be no other way, and hence we will let you have your wish. Only even without this, believe me, I will always remain your friend, and expect the same from you." — The others submitted the same wishes and declarations, and thus an alliance of friends was concluded which arose from fuller hearts than many which had been tied with full glass or at other occasions.

Gomphardt sat down, when he was alone, to his diary, and expressed in it his resolve to leave Hm. and to visit other towns. "The big world", he wrote in it, "has had a benevolent effect on me. My sorrow, without vanishing, is losing its bitterness, and I am again receptive to many impressions of joy. If other towns exercise a similar influence on me, then Amalie's memory will become a beneficial need for me."

The next day he revealed to Riccort his decision to depart and, in order to see other towns at a good time of year, not to hesitate any longer. Riccort wanted at first to hear nothing of it, but when he perceived his friend's seriousness, he said, "Our doctrine and way of life is driving you away, I should have noticed it long ago. But believe me, you will not find it better than here anywhere else. I know the world and know on what peaks it struts around, but mostly it does not see the street on which the honourable world citizen strolls. We have the golden middle of the road and worry less about such things than those who live merely for heaven, still less than such as who stick to the earth like the worm. A little heaven and the proper dose of earth gives a good drink on which body and spirit refresh themselves. This is our freemason and world citizen philosophy which, since we are all well as a result of it, must be the true one. You cannot make up your mind on such a doctrine and are having us pay for the zeal to draw you into our brotherly circle through your departure."

Gomphardt interrupted him here and said, "I make you pay for something! How can you come to such thoughts? If my seriousness does not always agree with your cheerfulness, then it lies in the nature of the thing. Grief took a hold of me, joy a hold of you; for this reason sometimes differences of form, but never of matter must arise. Friendship has been established between us and connects us, hopefully not only for the field of view of our eyes, but for all places and life circumstances."

Riccort had become noticeably serious at these words, seized Gomphardt's hand, and said, "You are better than we are. The free nature in which you lived kept the unhealthy air from your heart, whereas we, guided by doctrine and convenience, seldom look at the matter with natural eyes, mostly through glasses."

Gomphardt revealed to Riccort the wish to have all his acquaintances around him for an evening meal, and asked him to write down their names and to take over a part of the arrangements so that nothing would be forgotten and nobody overlooked. Riccort was pleased by this intention and promised to undertake everything in order to make it as complete as possible. The day was established, the friends invited, and see there, a company gathered of some forty and more persons.

Riccort had taken over the office of master of ceremonies and took care of everything with a decency and a punctuality that left nothing to be wished for. The most expensive dishes succeeded one another on the table, the empty bottles were replaced by full ones, and thus the company was, before the strike of midnight, in a mood which could not have been more cheerful. The champagne which was brought out in quantity loosened the tongues which had previously kept quiet into maxims and toasts which deserved to be recorded. But since the pen for such a loud company leads to too quiet a language, it can only be noted that Gomphardt received the most unfeigned proof of their friendly dispositions and finally felt forced to express his thanks in the following way.

"I drink in thanks for your love and friendship. I came to you from the countryside without the fine manners of the city, and nevertheless you have honoured me often through your obliging kindness. Never in my life have I forgotten kindnesses; therefore my nature would have to change if what thanks I am obliged to you should ever escape my memory. I drink to what I will feel through my entire life — the thanks for your friendship and kindness."

He emptied his glass almost to the dregs amidst the joyful shouts of the company.

They stayed together until long after midnight, and before they parted, each requested permission to be permitted to show him a favour, be it by a small gift or memento, or by the addresses of important houses in those towns which he was intending to visit. He accepted the addresses, but he promised to fetch the gifts himself when he came to this district again. Everybody went home cheerful, and they spoke for a long time afterwards about the delights of this evening.

The next day Riccort came to Gomphardt and said, "Since your departure has been decided and is not to be pushed off anymore, we, my friends and I, are in agreement in providing you with such addresses that you will certainly be able to promise yourself the best reception in every city in Germany. In such a way that you will be required to remember us and remain connected to us at least in thought." Gomphardt felt moved by such unfeigned concern and said, "You, you and your friends, indeed all those with whom I came into contact here, are so good and kind that it is almost impossible to be so accepted in another place, and if my life path allows me to reside in a town, then I would choose my present residence over all others. Only I must go, learn to examine the forms and the worth of life with others too in order to see whether I will finally succeed in winning a firm standpoint and a certain outlook."

Riccort replied, "To this end I will give you, since you intend travelling to Bl., a letter of introduction to my friend Reiner, who knows how to explain everything we have previously discussed here according to the rules of reason, and how to resolve the cause and aim of all the spiritual and physical phenomena as thought it were simple arithmetic. He works the same field as we do, that is, he is a freemason, but the fruits which he draws, or hopes to draw, are of a different nature. He gives us the shameful name of indifferentists, who are hardly to be seen as half-born, but as the main cause of the corruption amongst humanity. He believes not only in immortality and reward and punishment in the hereafter, he knows this; reason has explained and proven everything to him, and hence he calls his artificially constructed system faith in reason. You will get to know and respect him, but at the same time be surprised at how he understands how to demonstrate everything and only regrets not being able to initiate the entire world into his doctrine."

After they had conversed for some more time, both parted, Riccort to a business friend outside the town, Gomphardt to make his farewell visits.

The day of departure arrived, and Gomphardt left with a peculiar melancholy feeling the town where he had enjoyed so many demonstrations of friendship. He travelled slowly in order to get to know both the area and its state of culture, and only arrived on the eighth day at Bl., where he felt somewhat uncomfortable when he caught sight of the palaces, uniforms, state coaches, and a number of things which had previously been foreign to him.

***

The Faith in Reason

Gomphardt entered the Hotel de N. H., one of the leading guesthouses of the city, and had allocated to himself, according to his needs, three rooms, two for himself and one for his servant. His wish was fulfilled though in a way as though one was accustomed here to only taking in the leading notables of the world, merely reserving a place for a sole traveller on the other hand out of a sort of generosity. The rooms were incidentally elegant and appropriately furnished, and Gomphardt, resolved to linger in Bl. for some time, began immediately to order everything for his comfort.

A waiter came with the hotel register and had the proper notes entered, but did not ask whether the new guest wanted to eat, drink, stay, or leave. To our traveller this manner of treating him gave him a strange feeling, and the comparisons which he made with the reception in Hm. turned out very much to the disadvantage of his current landlord. But he soon ignored it, for we read in his diary, in which he still expresses his feelings today, the following in this respect.

Rural, moral.
I have sought humans and found forms.
What surely would the human be if he could dispose of all foreign forms and appear in his natural state? This question has already occupied many people, occupies still many more, and will unfortunately not be answered as soon as would be desirable with sufficient thoroughness.

The next day he dressed carefully, sat himself in an elegant carriage of his landlord's, had himself accompanied by a stately hired servant, and made visits to a few notables, bankers, and significant trading houses, submitted the letters of credit and of introduction which he had brought along, and was received everywhere with big city courtesy, which he could not yet come to terms with and often did not know whether he had on his side perhaps done too much or too little.

"The form makes us embarrassed, often even confused," he said to himself when he was again in his room. "I know their forms as little as they know mine, and hence it will be best if each sticks to his own way and trusts in the good-naturedness and natural acumen of the other."

Gomphardt continued making visits on the following days, and when he was at an end with it, he wrote to Riccort and explained to him the difference of his current residence with his earlier one in Hm.

"Friend!", it said in his letter, "You cannot imagine how strange I feel here. All with whom I come into contact are so deft and finished that it often seems to me as if I did not yet possess the first rudiments of life. Our believer in reason, Doctor Reiner, I have not yet been able to speak with. I did indeed visit him, but found him overweighed with business to such an extent that I immediately left again after handing over your letter. He returned my visit, but could not, on account of lack of time, get involved in any conversation with me. 'In the coming weeks', he said, 'I will be free and will exert everything to make your stay here as pleasant as possible.'

Friend! The exterior of your believer in reason pleases me. He seems to me, without offending anyone, to be the most rational one here."

Gomphardt's acquaintances increased significantly after a few weeks. He was introduced into circles of artists, scholars, and writers, and found here for the first time that even art and literature were treated just as professionally as any other business. "It is not easy to know the world," he wrote on this point in his diary. "For someone who does not see behind the curtain of a thing, it seems to them they are in a half darkness which often attunes us to awe; but as soon as the curtain is drawn back, we see the objects in their true light, and the halo of holiness and of awe vanishes."

Gomphardt had meanwhile made the closer acquaintance of Doctor Reiner. The latter came to him in the guesthouse one day and invited him to a party in the countryside the next day at which several of his friends would be gathered. Gomphardt naturally accepted the invitation and asked the Doctor whether he would be permitted to drive to his house beforehand and fetch him. The latter replied that he would not have the pleasure taken from him of providing for and attending to his guest the next day with respect to everything concerning the party. Gomphardt could do nothing but reply to this courteousness with the proper thanks and leave himself to the disposition of his patron.

The day arrived. Doctor Reiner arrived in an elegant, magnificently harnessed carriage before Gomphardt's hotel, and after he had taken up his guest and travelled for about three quarters of an hour at a sharp trot, he said, as they were coming to a standstill before a large house almost completely surrounded by a garden, "We are there. Nature has not done much for our area; art must help everywhere; hence I ask you not to extend your expectations too far and to take into account the goodwill with which we entertain guests."

Reiner led his guest into a room opening onto the garden where a party of seated men were in groups in the process of of making loud conversation. They greeted the arrivals with hurried decency and for the greatest part continued their conversations where they were. Reiner introduced a few of the members of the company who had joined him to the traveller, Mr Gomphardt, who had been recommended to him by a trusted friend, and thus the time passed amidst mutual greetings and conversations until the midday meal was carried out. They ate and drank, spoke in small pauses about everything which the events of the day offered, over achievements in the fields of drama, music, painting, sculpture, poetry, and urban beautification. No branch of human knowledge and capability remained untouched, and you would have immediately been able to become aware that here a select society had gathered from all classes and branches of business.

After the end of the meal, the conversation took a specific direction. Reiner now took the opportunity of describing his guest to the company more precisely and saying that he was expressly recommended by his friend Riccort from Hm. to familiarise him with the principles of the faith in reason and to give him thereby the life's support again which he had lost through his troubles. Immediately he brought attention to Mr Gomphardt being, indeed not a member of freemasonry, but by contrast instructed by frequent consort with members of the order so much that you could speak without regard to ceremony about any subject frankly. Everybody was pleased by this visit and gave the assurance of doing their utmost to justify the expectations that had been nursed. One expressed his astonishment at how Riccort, such a decided indifferent-ist, had sent them a student and not preferred to have kept him himself. Another responded, "Riccort is too rational not to see that his indifferentism does not suffice and floats like a mist in low hills where you never know the moment when it will dissolve and fall to earth as drops of water."

"Reason in its free activity", he continued speaking, "is that light which preserves us and gives us independence in all the circumstances of life. Just as it is in a position to illuminate all that is visible, it is also capable of penetrating into the regions of invisible activities and investigating the basic cause of all being. Nothing can arise with will and without plan. The will is the uppermost characteristic of reason, and the plan is the model drafted in reason for some activity or creation. If these two clauses must be recognised as being infallible, then all other conclusions follow necessarily of themselves, and the human sees himself led to the conviction of his destiny almost without knowing how he came to it.

The first clause is: the will is the uppermost characteristic of reason. For the limited thinker this claim seems to be a paradox because he is accustomed to seeing reason in no other way than when it collects ideas, forms concepts, estab-lishes judgements, and draws conclusions. Only when we consider that without free will, without a law for the activity of this, nothing could take place, we are thus required to bring will and the power of thought under one idea and to say: without will we cannot think and without thinking we cannot want."

Here the talker was interrupted by stormy calls of acclaim, and Gomphardt himself, to whom the matter was new, could not conceal that thoroughness and consistency had ruled in the talk, and concurred in the applause with honest heart. When calm had been established again, the talker continued.

"The task of philosophy is to provide information about God and immortality. Any philosophy which does not do this is not a philosophy, but rather a seduction which blinds the listener under the aegis of a dedicated name and gives them haze instead of truth. We do not want to misuse philosophy for any lower aims, rather we want to get to know through its light our reason and through reason get to know the keystone of philosophy — God and immortality.

The goal we know — God and immortality. The means we likewise know — power of thought and free will. Reason consists of power of thought and will, as we have already heard. Reason is accordingly of a dual nature and also in this way active, for it drafts the plan and executes it as will at the same time. In any plan, however, there lies a yet further goal which is actually to be considered as the main motif of the activity of reason. From this it emerges that each effect must have two causes, of which one encloses in itself the goal, the other the power that brings forth. If it were any different, then we would have to see each activity only as a boy's game where he leaps over the ditch as the result of an urge, but has no cause as his goal. Thus would be the activity of God, if it were to have created humanity without the cause of a goal. But since the human was created in all perfection, the plan of creating him so and in no other way must have had a cause as consequence laid at its foundation, which can be none other than to fan the light of reason in humanity and to have it then shine eternally in the eternal regions of reason."

New applause followed this conclusion. One person could not comprehend how it was possible to misjudge such truths and not accept them as the basic cause of religion. "With such confessions of belief", one said, "a war of religion would never have arisen." Another claimed, "Only with such views can humanity be raised to the peak of all knowledge." A third asked for permission to explain in respect to religion and the cited basic principles and to be permitted to illuminate them from another side. After he had received the agreement of the company, he began.

"The apostle Paul, the greatest light of the New Testament doctrine and the most zealous spreader of the Christian religion, said in his first epistle to the Thessalonians: Prove all things; hold fast that which is good*. Can such an expression suggest anything but a religion of reason? Certainly not. If we therefore explain our doctrine as being in complete agreement with Christianity, then we do so under the authority of the greatest Christian teacher. Furthermore we read in the Bible, that absolutely canonical book, that God made man in his own image — in the image of God†. Many struggle to fathom the meaning of these words; on the path of reason it is cleared up completely. Reason is the most perfect thing which the human knows; we therefore cannot think of God in any other way than under the idea of the highest reason. God is the highest reason, is the epitome of it; he creates beings which likewise possess reason and are therefore like him, are his own image. But for reason it is not enough to support itself on authorities and to thereby establish its truths; it draws from itself and establishes laws of nature which no doctrine and no sophistry is capable of knocking over. 'How does it surely proceed here?', some will ask. In the simplest manner in the world. It begins with itself and says: the human possesses me, he is rational, hence is one with me. Where does reason come from though? Can accident or unreason have given it to him? Certainly not. As little as the flowers obtain brilliance and adornment without the colours of sunlight, just as little can the human receive reason if an eternal sun of reason does not stand over creation and fill us with its light. We see from that that the human, even when we go beyond him and rise to the creator, finds the truth of the Bible confirmed where it says the human is an image of God. Since now God on his own and in full power can have no end, his image, which is at the same time a part of him, must thus

---

*   [Tr.: 1 Thessalonians 5:21.]

†   [Tr.: cf. Genesis 1:27.]

necessarily enter into communion with him and be immortal like he is. From such foundations the faith in reason rests on God and immortality."

General thanks and applause were then accorded to the speaker. Gomphardt himself was surprised by the thorough build-up of ideas and expressed his beliefs about it aloud. "I consider myself obligated", he said, "to my patron, to Doctor Reiner, to express my warmest thanks for the good deed of having led me into your company. The words faith in reason usually stand with all who hear or say them in such a bad light that I myself expected nothing else but Platonic dialogue developed in the finest way, combined with sentimental Christian ideas in order to also satisfy the heart alongside the understanding; instead of which basic concepts are set up and analysed in a way that I feel myself forced to give recognition to my admiration and to ask you to let me also take further part in these instructive meetings."

A loud cry of joy from the company followed this hearty expression of thanks. Everybody filled their glasses and emptied them with pleasure over the presence of such a welcome guest.

A pause occurred in which each person was drawn into a special conversation with their neighbour in order to recall once more what had just been heard. It was time to think of returning home, and many went by and by to the host so as to also gratify him. As this was happening and a number of the carriages stood already harnessed before the house, one of those present requested to speak in order to establish the received impressions of truth yet more firmly. Everybody gathered once more around the table and he spoke.

"We gathered here today in the light of reason, and it has illuminated us. It cannot be extinguished anymore, provided that we only to some extent follow nature and espy in it the spirit of the creator. It, the great mother, stands in unmistakeable truth before us and unveils to us all the secrets of the present and future. Look just at how full it is of the eternal spirit which develops itself in countless forms and beauties and commands us to believe in it. When I speak here of faith, I do not mean the visible form, but rather the spirit poured from eternity which raises itself into visibility. Reason cannot draw results from the spirit, the invisible, but it can infer from the visible the invisible, open through this ability the gates of eternity and recognise God and immortality.

Everything is full of spirit, starting from God and returning again to him. The light draws the spiritual powers from the candle and sends them as flames into the ether. The flower adorns itself with colour and brilliance, not for the earth, but rather for the higher regions of light. Colour and brilliance are nothing else but the light on the candle. In this image we can also recognise the activity of the animal kingdom, even of humanity. Instinct and drive are lights on the candle; under-standing, reason, and freewill are also no different, they are only of such a holy and pure sort that we often step back in astonishment and only timidly make an attempt at their investigation. What once develops into the spiritual cannot become dust anymore; it flies heavenwards, to its home. Can the wine return to its grape? Can it be turned into earth? Nevermore! It is preserved with care for the welfare of humanity. Even if you spilt it onto the street, its spirit would rise upwards and merge with pure matter. Thus is everything in nature. Thus too reason in the human. It is something positive, is a light on a living candle which, even if the candle breaks, flies up to the eternal throne of wisdom in order to shine there itself and enter into purer knowledge for life. This little bit yet for the praise of reason and in thanks for the lectures which we heard today."

Loud applause sounded, and everybody parted in the feeling of a happy and blissfully spent day. Gomphardt travelled again with Reiner, who brought him to the guest-house and left him with the request to now be completely at his disposal, and with the assurances of the friendliest relations.

Gomphardt was quite spellbound by the impressions of the current day. The thought of reducing beliefs to bases of reason and finally learning to believe through reason, was something so new and enticing for him that he devoted himself completely to it. Even when he went to his diary in the evening, he did not have the uninhibitedness to give his feelings and thoughts a calm hearing, and sufficed with speaking about the diversity of human arrangements and deriving from this the variety of views and life systems.

The next day he made a return visit to his friend, Doctor Reiner, and was inexhaustible in his praise over the tone and the tendencies of the company the previous day. He asked to be permitted to attend such gatherings as often as possible and to count him as one of them, with whatever sacrifices and expenditures it might also be connected. Reiner was pleased at this proposal, and replied, "It is particularly in our times, when you often consider under the mantle of religiosity or of reason that the appearance is the truth, that quickness is strength, and lack of restraint is freedom, very comforting to find men who renounce prejudices and give themselves over to the single true guidance. Sacrifice and expenditures, there are none because we need no locale of our own and wherever we find ourselves, the altar of our association stands."

Gomphardt asked in what way it was possible to bring together such an exceptional company.

Reiner replied, "Through freemasonry."

Gomphardt: "Through freemasonry?"

Reiner: "None other. In the temples of this association are gathered, even if not utter heroes of virtue, always though the most excellent people of a town or area, where the like-minded are found and unite without laws or statutes, often without wanting them, to a special end and work towards it unchallenged by the rest."

Gomphardt: "Freemasonry is a remarkable institution by which, in whatever circumstances you come into contact with it, it acts beneficially and makes us familiar with phenomena which we could never have seen without it."

Reiner: "That is indeed directly the primary aim of the institution, to gather and to seek, not only knowledge and learnedness, but rather like-minded hearts with which you can connect and strengthen yourself in the striving for en-noblement and truth."

Gomphardt: "I am astonished and almost beginning to regret having given my word not to become a freemason."

Reiner: "Every educated man should be a freemason, not in order to learn something new, something positive, but rather to find from the mass of members his true brothers who harmonise with him."

Gomphardt became contemplative and was already half resolved to ask the Doctor to write to the Deacon in his name and ask him for the return of his word; only he controlled himself in order to not endanger through the authority of a commitment the freedom of his own research. Reiner noticed his contemplation and said, "You seem upset about what I have said."

Gomphardt: "Why should I conceal it from you? I am considering whether it could be beneficial for me to enter into the society of freemasons."

Reiner: "And over that you are still uncertain?"

Gomphardt: "Allow me to ask, is Riccort, the neutral one, the indifferentist, just as good a freemason as you and your friends?"

Reiner: "Quite certainly."

Gomphardt: "And Rinkam, the historian?"

Reiner: "Likewise."

Gomphardt: "And Reinthal, the propagandist?"

Reiner: "He seeks and gathers feelings of brotherhood in the order."

Gomphardt: "And you and your friends?"

Reiner: "Are seeking according to the laws of reason the proof of immortality."

Gomphardt: "And all this happens on the initiative of freemasonry?"

Reiner: "In that the like-minded find themselves in it, yes."

Gomphardt: "Accordingly freemasonry would have no aim of its own, only the aims of those coming to it?"

Reiner: "Is to you what has been said not a sufficient aim?"

Gomphardt: "It would have nothing of which it could say, 'That belongs to me alone! That no other institution works on!"

Reiner: "No other institution possesses such universality."

Gomphardt: "A universality of splintering, where none can say of the others, he is my brother for the sake of the affair which we carry on? Must such a universality reaching into all branches not become dangerous in the end?"

Reiner: "I do not believe so."

Gomphardt: "Can it not in the end get mixed up in the institutions of state and general religious customs?"

Reiner: "If it happens in moderation, it will not harm."

Gomphardt: "But who determines here moderation?"

Reiner: "The laws of the federation."

Gomphardt: "And are such always effective enough?"

Reiner: "In an ordered state, yes."

Gomphardt: "But in a disordered one?"

Reiner: "It may admittedly give some concerns."

Gomphardt: "And who is the judge who can tell us always with reliability whether the the state is ordered or not?"

Reiner: "In other lands irregularities have occurred in this respect; with us such a thing is not to be feared."

Gomphardt: "I believe it myself and thank you for your willingness to instruct me."

Doctor Reiner, who had preserved a certain stiffness in these questions and answers, feared Gomphardt might see in him a maker of proselytes and said, "My utterances seem to alienate you, and yet I was not in a position to give you different information. Had freemasonry something positive which it could establish as doctrine, then it would do so in that it would certainly be better off as a result, than steering about on such an immeasurable ocean where it often sees no place to anchor. But since it is no different, we must take the matter as it appears and must draw as much good from it as possible. Meanwhile do not let what has been said trouble you and just believe that we always know how to treasure a bold investigator of truth, even without the warrant of a brother."

Gomphardt apologised as well as he could, and asked him not to take offence at his perhaps exaggerated concerns. "They are not concerns which you utter", Reiner replied, "but rather wishes which express them. You desire from freemasonry something positive, independent, something which only it possesses and can share. That is not to be found at all according to the way it is conducted in most lodges. Indeed I do not want to deny whether something of the sort could not be contained in it; for there is amongst its symbols many which, to be regarded merely as signs of recognition, reach far too deeply into nature. Until now only a few lodges have attempted to give the external arrangements some deeper meaning. I cannot therefore, as I already noted earlier, give you any information about this, but promise that as soon as I obtain knowledge about a positive treatment, I will share it with you and leave to your discernment the judgement over it."

This discussion had brought forth a little tension amongst the two conferring, but without reducing the mutual interest which they took in one another. Reiner therefore made the suggestion to go out and take a look at a few of the curiosities of the town. He led him to the ateliers of two distinguished artists, a walk which, on account of the novelty, was of great interest. "The arts", said Reiner, "are the inseparable companions of reason, because they realise the ideas of it and portray them vividly."

The viewing of significant artworks warmed up their dispositions again, and they spoke afterwards for a long time about the aims of human nature and the means of recognising them. Gomphardt asked the Doctor to organise a gathering again soon, like the previous one, and offered to bear all the costs for it. Reiner promised to fulfill his wish, but without accepting his offer with respect to costs. Three days later Reiner's friends gathered in a guesthouse in the town, and Gomphardt had the pleasure of joining them as an old acquaintance and already discussing in advance with a few of them the lectures to be expected.

It would be going too far to share everything which was said and recited on this evening, enough, Gomphardt felt, like at the first gathering, enthused by the novelty of the ideas, the adroitness of the talk, and especially by the seriousness and zeal which reigned in the talks, and expressed his thanks and his admiration aloud again. But when a few members of the company called upon him to connect even more closely with them and become a freemason, he gave evasive answers with the intimation of considering the matter. The company parted incidentally very edified; but Gomphardt made a note to be on his guard, despite his admiration.

Members of another lodge had also already made his acquaintance and learnt that he had already often visited Reiner's get-togethers, without though deciding on taking up freemasonry. They considered it to be a good sign, and made some attempts to win him for themselves. "Reiner's system of reason", they said, "cannot please such a clever and intelligent man; such a one does not want any demonstrations of reason, but rather practical views." They now made their plans, sought to make him aware of a more real sense of freemasonry, and one by the name of Klinkof, a jurist, undertook to win him for his party. To this end he dined a few times at Gomphardt's guesthouse, got involved in conversation with him as often as was possible, and when they were not yet at the end of a topic one day, Klinkof went with him to his room and sought to guide the discourse they had begun imperceptibly towards freemasonry. Since Gomphardt always answered evasively over this subject, he asked him, "Are you a freemason though?"

Gomphardt: "No."

Klinkof: "That amazes me, since all educated people make it their task and set great store in becoming members of a lodge."

Gomphardt: "To follow others in practical life, I find to be proper; in life views, I consider each to be obligated in the main to themselves."

Klinkof: "Quite right. But a little connecting thread is not superfluous in such respects either."

Gomphardt: "You may be right. It depends though on whether freemasonry knows how to give such a connecting thread."

Klinkof: "It gives the norm according to which our ancestors went to work."

Gomphardt: "That is a lot, if the norm is genuine."

Klinkof: "It is, the undoubted documents and constitutions vouch for it."

Gomphardt: "And what do these teach?"

Klinkof: "How our fathers instituted, conducted, and preserved their gatherings."

Gomphardt: "But to what aim?"

Klinkof: "To the aim of self-ennoblement in that you accustom yourself to honouring given laws and to fulfilling them according to an open contract."

Gomphardt: "The fulfilment of laws was thus the aim?"

Klinkof: "None other."

Gomphardt: "I was taught every law was given for the achieving of a goal and could never itself be a goal."

Klinkof: "In common life, certainly."

Gomphardt: "With you it is accordingly different. You will forgive me if I find this strange. But perhaps I do not yet comprehend the matter and therefore I shall ask for closer instruction."

Klinkof: "If I tell you in the same way as we were told, the freemasons had already gathered a hundred years ago and revealed themselves; still more, already in the year 926 the first solid constitutions were founded and the laws of the second century taken for the guiding principle; you will thus not find it anything but extremely interesting to use the same manners, sentences, and movements as happened in those times."

Gomphardt: "If such manners, sentences, and movements do not aim at any specific goal, if no results were to be obtained thereby, then I deplore our ancestors for be able to get involved in such games; but I cannot praise us when we have continued such games for centuries."

Klinkof: "You have accordingly no sense for antiquities?"

Gomphardt: "If they have historical, positive value, or if you can learn something thereby, oh yes. But tell yourself, what would you think of a man who possessing the palette and brush of an Apelles*, and without being able to paint, or at least learn to paint, pretended to be a painter?"

Klinkof: "I don't see where these questions are supposed to lead."

Gomphardt: "They are supposed to lead to the effect that, so long as the world stands, constitutions and laws are always given for reaching a goal that one has in sight. The goal can from the beginning on never arise from external forms and laws, it was always the goal to whose attainment constitutions and laws were established. The military has military laws in order to make it efficient for defending the fatherland in an emergency and striking its enemies. Laws of state are present in order to promote the goals of the state, industry and welfare, order and public spirit, morality and humanity. The

---

* [Tr.: Apelles was an acclaimed 4th century B.C.E. Greek painter.]

98

freemasons, however, seem to have raised the law to a goal, enjoy antique forms, entertain the enclosure of the well, unconcerned whether the spring itself flows or not. Indeed, they would, me thinks, dig out the source if it accidentally still flowed, just in order to not be reminded to draw from it. Show me the source! Make me familiar with the goal, and if this seems beneficial to me and important enough, I will accept your suggestion thankfully."

Klinkof saw after this answer that he would not reach his goal so easily here, asked therefore for forgiveness for having been tiresome for so long, and left with the intention of not making any further attempt here.

Gomphardt went the next day to Reiner and gave him a report of Klinkof's visit and his intention to move him to enter his lodge. Reiner allowed himself to be informed precisely and said, after he had heard everything, "It is incomprehensible how the most educated and rational of men can play with such magnificent forms without suspecting or seeking a kernel behind it. The scholarly and artificially put together tirades over the origin of the association, constitutions, signatures, and thousands of other things have distanced us so far from the matter that, even if it were also found again, it would have to be dangerous to touch it and express it clearly. Had I not the most grounded of suspicions that something beneficial for all of humanity would have to be contained in the forms and symbols of freemasonry; if it did not give me the opportunity to find like-minded members amongst them and to at least gather them about myself for a rational goal; truly, I would reproach myself for deadening my time through empty ceremonies and convince myself at the same time of the weakness of human power of thought. But enough of that. Let us speak about our own affairs.

My friend Riccort gave me a report over you which takes up my entire interest in you. He knows how much I go to battle against his indifferentism, by comparison taking sides with everything in which a certain firmness, a positive or even only ideal aim is made perceptible. You entrusted him with your life history and thereby with the reason for your rift with yourself, but did not want, despite the efforts which he made for your sake, to decide to accede to his views and to join with him to this end. This brought him, by virtue of his natural kind-heartedness, to the decision to address you to me. You are here, have seen the fruits of my endeavours to attain through reason a positive life goal. To begin with I believed to have won you over entirely to our views; but the thoughtfulness which you let show after a few of our meetings soon convinced me that I had miscalculated, and that you also do not find with us what you are seeking."

Gomphardt's affability, which could never bring him to fob off with prevarications someone who was showing himself to be obliging, came as a result of this declaration into a not inconsiderable embarrassment. He wanted to answer. But Reiner did not let him speak, and said, "Do not let yourself worry about my open-heartedness, and think rather that it will be more expedient for us to get to know each other without subterfuge. I know your life history, so have in respect to the judgement of your character much of an advantage over you; I will, so as to put us in a proper parallel, make you familiar with my life history too and then leave it to your judgement whether you will accompany me further on my path, or strike a different track for your investigations.

I am the only son of a respected state official who married through my mother into significant wealth. My father, an exceedingly respected man, experienced in all business circumstances, had me given an education the like of which only a few are granted. In my youth I had the best private tutors. When I entered high school though, there everything was applied completely to laying a good foundation for my future scientific education. I enjoyed learning, and learnt easily; hence it came about that I had acquired the background knowledge a few years earlier than the age allowed for going to university. This time was of course not permitted to pass unused, hence I had language teachers not only in living, but also in the old oriental languages. I seemed to people, in respect to what I had learned by heart, to be a sort of wonder, and hence it became probable that my father afterwards, regardless of the so-called money subjects, seemed to have no other intention than to make from me a complete academic. I was indeed registered as a law student; only I dedicated the greatest part of my time to the study of history and to the philosophical and mathematical sciences, so that I had to complete five years before I could pass my law exams. This turned out against all expectations, through the philosophical order which I knew how to put into it, so well that I would have been justified in applying straightaway for a position in the civil service. I could not make up my mind on that; but in order to do something, without though offending my affection for the sciences, I then registered myself in the list of legal practitioners as an advocate.

From then on, although I still lived in my parents' house, my behaviour received an independence which I had not known previously. As a student you always stand under the oversight not only of the father, but also of the mother, and this forms a relationship of a child-like nature which belongs with the years of study. I was so fortunate in my business that I had to turn away many requests, but had the misfortune of losing my parents in the space of three years. How much of an influence this loss has had on my subsequent way of thinking, I do not know; enough, the tendency towards speculative philosophy gained the upper hand in me so that I resolved to live for it entirely and where possible to investigate its highest principle, its final goal, without all the deceptive side-branching and without the compulsion of any one school.

What is philosophy? That was of course in my state at the time the first and most important question. I sought in all the contemporary philosophical systems, but could not find a definition as I wished it anywhere. In the older periods the philosophers were natural priests, and without philosophy no priesthood seemed conceivable. I followed this idea and I found myself in a short time in full conflict with the scholars of our time, with whom philosophy and religion stood there as quite separate subjects. Religion and philosophy had to be one according to the view I just expressed; how would it be possible to bring these two seemingly heterogeneous things under one idea?

I saw all the obstacles which towered up before me; but my resolve remained unshaken. The knowledge of those oriental languages now became very useful to me; I read the Zend in the original language, made myself familiar with the doctrine of the Brahmans and the Buddhists, with the symbols of the magi and Egyptians, and in order to have done everything, I studied the Bible, compared it with other writings and found that, if the religions were not to be traced back to one highest principle, then there could be no talk of one highest principle for philosophy at all.

To treat religion as philosophy, and philosophy as religion was the task now, whose solution especially borders on the impossible in these days in which the one seems to exclude the other. But even if not the slightest outlook for a satisfying result was present, the matter remained too important to me to not happily dedicate all my powers to it. That I did, and since I did not find any more sources from which I could draw, I thought of freemasonry. I had read much about this institution and noted intimations from which you could conclude there was something elevated which agreed with my task. I applied to be accepted, received entry, and to begin with it seemed as if my wishes were to be satisfied. The sublimity of the ceremony, the years, the founder or patron and other circumstances filled my disposition with the most beautiful hopes. But in a few years I already recognised the deception which I had entertained. I received by and by all the degrees, but yearned from one to the other in vain for information. Morality, humanity, brotherly love, and philanthropy were the topics which were taught from every pulpit, and often even much better than in the freemasons' halls, about which nevertheless the lectures of the members turned like a wheel without though leaving behind in their bourgeois life clearer traces than we see with other people.

Humanity often loses itself in selfish, often political views; morality, however, was a separation from all positive, religious statutes; philanthropy is a Biblical law presented in the Christian religion and resting in the heart of the human, and it needs no special institution in order to teach us it, it would have to be then that we were considered children to whom the will of the father must be repeated daily. Brotherly love is an actual basis on which society rests. This law is practised in the most various ways. To those addicted to pleasure there is the convenience of finding brothers everywhere, even when he enters a guesthouse, with whom he can converse. To the scholar it creates connections with all the lands and opens to him the way of entering into this or that scholarly society and receiving a diploma as honorary member. To merchants the advantage dawns of thereby making acquaintances in the simplest way and establishing trading business. The artist finally receives through the members of the institution adherents and spreaders of his name so that he usually receives the advantage in competition with non-masons. This it was which was brought home to me factually as being the bias of freemasonry, and I would have long since withdrawn if the above described advantage of finding good men and of gathering them about oneself had not held me yet. For this reason alone I considered it the duty of any man of integrity to have himself taken into the order so as to provide to the truly good a counterbalance to half-heartedness, ambition, and vain seeking after pleasure.

This is certainly an extremely subordinate goal for a thinking man; only so long as no higher goal is found, you must satisfy yourself with it. Certainly from many places voices are to be heard which bring to our attention a kernel, a positive independence and a light peculiar only to freemasonry, but these voices are yet much too weak against the crust of hierarchical customs to burst through it, and so I see myself still directed to my own powers which, I feel, do not suffice without the help of friends.

For eight years I have searched in freemasonry and found nothing but traces. Only, even these were lost again when I followed them in a scientific way. Freemasonry is, according to all I have heard and read about it, of a practical nature, from which you must know the means and the use of them in order to investigate the spirit of this institution. Meanwhile it seems for this use, even if not all, at least those lodges which I have had the opportunity to visit have lost the key.

To find again what was lost was now the task which I had to make my goal. But how and where now to seek? Philosophy and religion remain ever the two inextinguishable lights which shone for me in the chaos of my investigations. Thus I asked myself again: what goals do philosophy and religion have? And to where do the desires of all those who practise them aim? Indeed, to where do the desires of all humanity aim?

I had already long since recognised the necessity of a law under which the destinies of all stand, whatever religious confession they might belong too. I thus asked myself: what is this law? And gave myself the answer: belief. — But the second question was: how should you believe? Answer: rationally. — But what should I believe? With this question I tied the knots again firmer than ever; for the answer, if it should be derived from reason, turned out so trivial that it did not actually reward the effort of thinking about it.

What should you believe? This question must of course have been repeated for as long as the answer was lacking. Belief, provided it should be a happiness for the person, must agree with his desires. But what does the human mainly desire? What does he place above all the goods of the world? The ineradicable desire of the human is life. Give him the prospect of a happy, secure life, and his desires are satisfied. Everything is subordinate to this mighty urge, even the belief in God. Give the human a secure life without God, and he will not refuse it; but give him God without the security of his life, and he has lost the joys of his short existence already in advance. Now I had what I sought, namely the object of belief and indeed so open and undisguised that you could have been terrified of it. — Give the human a secure proof for immortality, and the tasks of all mysteries, all religions and schools are solved.

I felt happy to finally know for once definitely what is necessary for us. I spoke with a few of my friends who were receptive to such ideas and formed the club into which I introduced you. We have not been idle, have been investigating and testing, as you yourself heard; but unfortunately I must confess that I see myself in essence just as far from the goal as I was earlier. What my friends and I say about the matter is good and expedient for those who already have belief and who through our talks need only edify and strengthen themselves; for the unbelievers, for the dry men of understanding, on the contrary, they are empty words which sound like proofs, but leave behind no concept and no impression."

Gomphardt felt extremely surprised by these confessions. The agreement of views, the ardent desire of Reiner for a higher knowledge, his courage and his persistence drew Gomphardt's heart compellingly to itself, and after he had offered his hand to Reiner, he said, "I admire you! So much clarity and so much persistence you will seldom find together. If you consider me worthy of being your travel companion on the path you are taking, then count on me. I will, even if only striving for an ideal goal, remain steadfast in order to give you thereby a proof of my respect and friendship."

Reiner held Gomphardt's hand in his own and replied, "Friend, it is something more than an ideal goal which I am striving for. Those who wrote the Bible, who laid down an unending treasure of wisdom in it, and those who portrayed the story of the gospels vividly, they all must necessarily have had a basis, an intention and a goal. The bequest which we received from those high models is, even if we only judge it according to the literal meaning, of such sublime nature that we are required to venerate the compilers themselves as geniuses of humanity. They have established doctrines for the judgement of which we lack the key. This key, however, is to be found, it lies in the nature of the human; I suspect I feel it sometimes, but when I think to grasp it, it vanishes from my hands without me knowing in what way."

"Friend!", he continued, looking Gomphardt in the eye, "our same way of thinking over the important affairs of life already makes us natural friends; but we want to seal our bond with words in order to be always conscious of the end goal of it and to give it constantly new strength through the reminder.

The great need of humanity for happiness is the conviction of your persistence after this life.

The conviction in this respect is of a dual sort, either through belief or through proof.

Belief is no secure support, for it can desert us, as you have yourself experienced; hence everybody who loves humanity is obliged to seek or help to seek the proof.

To this goal we want to bind ourselves and remain friends through our entire lives. You are travelling through the world and will seek in writings and associations; I am going further down my road and will not let my zeal cool. Whichever of us two succeeds in discovering the proof, or even just the key to it, will immediately provide the report to the other and put the means in his hands for achieving the same knowledge."

Both vowed this and Reiner declared that he felt much easier now that he had rolled the confession of his inability from his heart.

***

The Friendship

We see Gomphardt through the bond of friendship with Doctor Reiner at a standpoint from which he was learning to see the world from a different side than before. Previously he had lived in the narrow circle of his personality where he judged all contacts with others only to the degree they affected him. Now the temple of humanity is being opened to him. He shall dedicate himself to an activity which surpasses the limits of individuality and which applies to all humans. He has recognised the task; but the position is still too new to him for it would be held against him if he did not yet know how to find his way in it and embraced with ardent desire every detail which was only somewhat to be connected with this generality.

The bond of friendship which he closed with Reiner is, although of noble nature, such a detail in that he had his eye on not just the goal of this friendship, but rather the person which awoke the feeling of friendship in him. Reiner was regarded by him to be the whole of, indeed, in a few moments to be the entirety of humanity, and hence it was often still difficult for him to elevate himself to equal flight with him and to judge the obligation undertaken in its full generality.

"I have become estranged from myself," he himself wrote in his diary, "and endeavour in vain to place my task clearly before my eyes. I have become estranged from myself like someone on an immense plain on which the view all around disappears into the clouds which seem to bound the earth. Only I feel that from such a generality encompassing everything only good can arise and I will endeavour to learn to survey it."

Once Gomphardt came to Reiner and said, "I am clear with myself. The independence to which you intended to raise me, I will attain with difficulty. I feel born to a sort of dependency for which the evidence is found in my life story, but I possess so much feeling for myself as to not subordinate myself to any lower goals, but rather to dare the highest to which my friend-ship commands me. You have noble intentions for me. You know my powers; but you must set me the goal and make it clear in my eyes so that the thought of being noticed by you and rewarded with friendly recognition accompanies me and makes me a loyal companion in your undertakings."

Reiner responded to this, "The powers we know and we also know the goal. This is not immortality itself, but rather the proof of it. Had we this, then the world would be more ordered and would not so easily go from one extreme to another like the swan on the lake, according to mood swimming sometimes to here, sometimes to there."

Gomphardt: "Anyone who has belief needs no proof."

Reiner: "But someone who has no belief? Can you force someone to believe? Still more, is a matter which we believe surely already true on account of the belief? We must not, if we want to be true to our word, place any conditions and nor have any forced on us. The need of humanity gives us the task; its most necessary need is the proof of immortality. In such a thing everyone would unite, would concentrate everyone, and like a great family would move hand in hand through life."

Gomphardt: "Is the possibility of such a proof thinkable?"

Reiner: "If immortality exists, then a proof of it must lie in nature. The human can recognise and give proof of all which happens around him and which affects him. Where he is not capable of this, there life stops for him, and death takes its place."

Gomphardt: "According to this, if no proof is present for it, no immortality would be possible!"

Reiner: "So it is."

Gomphardt: "And we would have to place more weight on the proof than on the matter itself?"

Reiner: "Because the matter arises for us first from the proof, admittedly."

Gomphardt: "The proof would thus be the actual palladium* for the welfare of humanity?"

Reiner: "In this lies everything, the independence of the human, his goal and his happiness. The scholar has through it a direction of thought and inquiry which does not let him go astray anymore, philosophy has a highest point to which it can tie its propositions and draw infallibility. Indeed, all institutions for the ennoblement of humanity, even the religions, but particularly the Christian religion, first receive through such a proof again life and meaning."

Gomphardt: "Religion itself gives proof according to the sayings of the theologians."

Reiner: "No, religion does not prove, but rather builds on a previous proof."

Gomphardt: "That is strange, and yet it must be true, otherwise the adherents of a religion and its priests could not themselves doubt."

Reiner: "Religion rests on a proof which we do not know anymore. Without previous proof, no religion would have been able to arise, no founder would have been able to bring it to life."

Gomphardt: "Are there characteristics of such a knowledge of the proof?"

Reiner: "The Urim and Thummim of the Israelites have been lost. The symbols of the incarnations of Vishnu are for us only ludicrous fables and folk tales. Even the incarnation of Christ is in our eyes a phenomenon which, because we do not have the capability anymore of comprehending it, we explain it as myth and as a composition of weak-minded fellow believers†. Anyone can deprive and deny with reason bragging weaklings, but only the calm thinker can comprehend. Only a few are in a position to investigate an important matter and to share it with others at the same time. But these should not be scared off by obstacles and petty concerns from seeking the truth, but rather, in consciousness

---

*　[Tr.: palladium is an archaic term for safeguard.]
†　[Tr.: cf. part 2 of Krebs, *Principles of the Bible* (2024).]

of working for the truth, obey the driving force of its power, and strive to draw forth the truth from all its veils."

Gomphardt: "You have placed a new sun on the horizon of my life! I thank you and repeat that I will under the aegis of friendship, your friendship, do everything which belongs to our goal. Only I feel that I must leave you in order to be true to our intentions. Your vicinity, the utterances of your friends, it all works together to infect my way of thinking and to bend me under its authority. I must, according to your remark, obtain it myself, the path which the first founders of religions and other institutions of wisdom walked, to seek it in myself in order thereby, as the theosophists say, to reproduce the lost paradise."

Reiner: "So it is. We have something lost to seek and to find again; the doctrines of all the wise men of history aim at that. And only now does it occur to me that freemasonry also speaks of something lost and found again. Well, then we will seek, and even if no reward is to be received for it, the feeling of having struggled for the highest thing shall reward us."

They discussed other, less important affairs and settled amongst other things on an itinerary and the time of departure. Gomphardt asked Reiner to be permitted to invite his friends to a supper in order to be able to be with them once more and perhaps hear new lectures. When Reiner wanted to make objections, Gomphardt said, "I parted in the same way in Hm. from Riccort's friends and took with me a pleasant memory. The current stay was ten times more important for me, and hence let me bring a small offering of thanks." Reiner finally gave in and said he would discuss with a few of his friends about the day of the gathering and provide him with an answer.

They parted, and Gomphardt thought about what he had heard with serious contemplation. In the evening, before he went to bed, he sat down to his diary and expressed in it the following.

4th October.

I have concluded a bond of friendship, but am being thrown on my own resources to fulfill my obligations to my friend. I must leave my friend and wander alone. Will I be able to surely? I also stood alone when my wife left me; but at the time I did not think of a striding forwards, but rather would have preferred to have crawled into a cave. Now I must not stand still after a solemn promise, but must advance towards a goal of whose reaching I also do not yet have the slightest prospect.

Immortality! Mysterious word! You are an inheritance of humanity, many say. Sometimes, when my feelings are awoken, I would like to force myself to believe it; but when I question reason, the entrance into eternity closes again, and a happy reunion becomes the schemes of a fantastic dreamer.

Religion delivers no proof of immortality; it does not concern itself with this — immortality is to it an axiom over which to speak would be as useless as over the brightness of the midday sun. Religion teaches us only to escape an unhappy continuation and to obtain a happy one.

Who wrote immortality into the soul of the founders of religion and ancient peoples? Or rather, how was it written into their souls? Reiner says: the proof of immortality has been lost. To that I ask: was immortality itself lost with the loss of the proof or of the axiom?

Here would be the field for a new dogmatism, and instead of saying belief is the power of creation of eternal life, you could say the proof awakens to life, and without proof death reigns.

Away with such wordplay, of which Reiner himself is not always free. I desire a factual truth which also remains true without explanation and does not suffer the tiniest loss through any definition and description.

I have never yet dared to examine the content of the lectures which I heard at that first gathering with Reiner's friends. I was to carried away by them, without knowing whether they had reality.

One said: reason consists of will and the power of thought in that we cannot think without will and cannot want without thinking.

Against this nothing is to be said. But when he claims: from the three basic causes of all that has become the certainty of immortality is to be concluded, then it is to be found with calm contemplation that the conclusion is too daring.

If the desire comes over me to play on my own piano, then I will order one. The desire to play is the main motive, the instrument maker the cause as power, and finally the instrument appears as effect.

If the creator created the human in order to collect powers of reason about himself, then the speaker's lecture has a some grounds for itself. But if God created heaven and earth in order to have humans, then the incarnation is the basic cause or the goal, and the human fulfils his destiny in the earthly life course.

The second speaker said the human is a light on a living candle which, even if the candle breaks, flies to its origin. What does this view give us for proof? Where was our ego, in the candle or in the light? If these separate, what happens with our personality? This question can be solved by whoever has the desire to; it cannot change my views.

Reiner is right. For those who possess belief such lectures are useless; they cannot now nor ever serve as proof.

I must wait for where it will come to me and can do nothing but give my word: under all circumstances to preserve the freedom of my judgement in order thereby to perhaps come to the activity of reason put in prospect by Reiner. —

He lay in bed with some agitation from the various ideas which he had taken in that day, and could not sleep for a long time on account of nothing but designs for the future. The next day, to obtain his uninhibitedness and calmness again, he made several visits in order to announce his impending departure and to make his farewells.

On the third day Reiner came to him with the news that his friends would on the day after the following obey the invitation to be sent to them and take supper with him. Gomphardt immediately ordered a room with the landlord, made the other necessary arrangements for the assigned evening and had the guests formally invited in his name.

The evening of the festive dinner appeared. The inn was extremely tastefully arranged, and the guests began already during the meal to make exaltations of praise for their magnanimous host. At the end of the supper, Gomphardt asked for permission to express to the honoured guests his thanks for the friendship shown to him, and said, "As much as I also feel urged to set out to you the feelings of my heart, I will not be in a position though to say that to you as I would wish. I came as a stranger to you, and nonetheless you let me take part in your gatherings in which you were developing your most secret thoughts. If this alone were already sufficient to fill me with unforgettable thanks, then this feeling climbs still higher when I consider that you spoke about things which would have to be the most important and most sacred to any rational and feeling person. I will take with me from this town a wealth of knowledge which I could not have obtained in any other place in the world, and for which I owe thanks only to your kindness and distinguished reception.

If I direct in this respect a few words to your leader, to the chair of your company, I am convinced that you will not disapprove of it, but rather will agree with me.

The idea of producing a belief in reason which does not emanate from circumventing the propositions of the reigning religion, or subordinating them, but rather from treating religion and philosophy as one matter, is so beautiful, great, and sublime that everybody must feel stirred to show him their thanks and their awe over it. And this I do with the explanation that I have not yet found anyone similar in the course of my life who with the setting aside of any temporal profit and any fleeting honour dedicates himself only to virtue and truth, and demonstrates that which he has recognised as good and true in his own life as well.To him my thanks are offered with the request to all his friends who are present here to support him in his striving as before and to walk by his side with love and zeal. What high worth he sets on your friendship and help, I alone know in that he has often expressed how charitable, indeed how necessary amiable participation is for him. A high as he stands, he looks though with thanks at you who have placed him so high, and hence I give to you, in that I am thanking him, at the same time the best testimony of my recognition of his worth and ask you, even if I will not be with you anymore, to think of me and to see me as a member of your association who sets reason up as an abiding light of life and, free from narrow-minded views, does not destroy, but places all that is good, true, and sublime under its aegis. I thank you in the heartiest and warmest way and empty my glass to the dregs as testimony of my love and thankfulness."

He drank and everyone responded to this toast with a triple hooray.

Several more toasts followed, which deserved to be recorded, but are passed over as not being essential to the matter. When it was already midnight, and the company was making moves to split up, Reiner took the lead and expressed himself thus, "When we speak truth, this is according to the usual view and also according to our own views an outflow of reason, and yet we experience in moments of the purest life's activity that the feelings have just as much share in such an outflow as the power of thought. And it is just that which distinguishes our gatherings from many others, that we strive to judge the human in his double potency, as creature of feeling and of reason. In an hour like today's, in an hour of the highest solemnity, where the heart gets in the way of the mind and asserts its claims, we actually stand at the most sublime point where we learn to recognise through the feelings and through knowledge for the first time how to feel truly human. I send this out ahead in order to bring to the attention of the venerable members that I feel myself forced today to let my feelings speak more than my mind.

Mr Gomphardt has allied to us with a warm, open heart. He has taken up the good things which he heard from us, but without following our authority blindly. His heart is entirely our own, even if his views are not yet entirely our own. He has, as befits the man, reserved his free judgement for as long as until irrefutable proofs determine him to change it. Such a disciple needs reason in that it possesses the ability of recognising itself, examining itself, and finding in the self-recognition its proofs. In this free and for us decisive sense, our new friend will be of essential use to the matter which we carry on and also, distant from here, will share with us the results of his investigations. He is leaving us and remains in spirit with us. He will see and hear other thinkers and will make us familiar with their views; in this way he has connected with us spiritually, and the bond of our mutual friendship cannot break so long as we are capable of thinking and of putting our thoughts into word-pictures.

I drink to him in the names of all as a farewell from our circle with these thoughts:

Our love and friendship accompanies him.

His love and friendship remains with us.

Love and friendship, purified by reason, are the lights of heaven which are never extinguished, and hence love and friendship are among us of eternal duration."

Everyone drank with enthusiastic agreement and demanded of Gomphardt that, wherever he might be, he should give them news from time to time and let them share in his progress. He promised to, and the gathering concluded at quite a late hour with repeated assurances of unwavering loyal convictions.

Gomphardt remained a further eight days in Bl. in order to make the necessary visits, to strengthen a few acquaintances, and mainly to discuss with Reiner the plan for his future activity. In this respect Reiner said, "You know what I am seeking, you also know my means, hence I cannot unveil anything more to you; but as much must I yet say, that I indeed suspect the existence of the possibility of the goal, that is, the possibility of finding a proof for immortality, but do not know yet how to give that proof. I have investigated everything, examined the institutions, in so far as history familiarises us with them, and only found one institution which still stands as a mysterious sphinx before my eyes, and that is freemasonry. In its ceremonies and symbols something is contained which only a few know and they preserve it as a self-gained property in order to perhaps not be misjudged or even mocked. And hence I command you, keep the freedom of your judgement.

Do not allow yourself to be taken in as a freemason until you have found one who tells you what it contains and teaches what distinguishes it from other institutions, and in what way it can be of use to humanity.

It must be one thing, not just a flowing together of many branches which grow together in the end and do not sprout any fruit anymore at all.

If you succeed in finding something on this path, then give me news straightaway so that I can obtain the opportunity of being active in it and helping the restoring of a long lost estate to humanity."

The day of departure arrived, and Gomphardt left Bl. fully strengthened in spirit and heart. The idea of humanity, a great whole, had found a place in him, and through that his individuality obtained a great yardstick which gave the feelings of his remaining grief a higher direction and often enclosed all of humanity in itself as being in the state of an essential loss.

***

The Humanists

Gomphardt came, after visiting a few smaller towns, to Br., where he had for the most part letters of recommendation. Fate ordained that such letters were mostly directed to freemasons, and so he saw himself, without being a member, by and by growing closer to the order in such a way that he often rued having bound himself in this respect. "But it is now so," he said in such moods to himself, "and I must keep all the more strictly to the fulfilment of my word as even Reiner's apprehensions commanded me to take care."

He delivered the recommendations brought with him, of which a letter of Reiner's to the justice Bonner obtained for him an especially good reception. This man knew Reiner from his university years and spoke with admiration of his distinguished talents and the magnanimity which had already animated him then and had now obtained such a high degree of strength.

Bonner could barely comprehend that Gomphardt had not already long since been taken up into the society of freemasons in that the bias towards it was already well known and necessary to every man of integrity and citizen of the world. Gomphardt excused himself by his perhaps too quickly given word, but asked his host to not withdraw his favour as a result and to provide him with the opportunity to become acquainted with the scientific and spirit-ennobling institutions of the town and to draw from that for his education as much advantage as possible.

Bonner rejoiced as these utterances and said, "Leave it to me! Whatever I am capable of shall happen, and I hope you will not rue having visited our town, which in many respects can be considered a model town. The university counts as its own excellent people. And amongst the other inhabitants there reigns such a spirit of humanity that everyone who is transferred to another place, even when it is to their advantage, feels unfortunate. Then the freemasonry possesses an influence here that you can plainly say gives the tone, and all societies are ordered and brightened by its spirit. I will speak with a few of my friends on your account, and if you want to be so kind as to visit me from time to time and make yourself at home in my household, then I hope I shall satisfy your expectations completely."

Gomphardt was in a short time introduced into all the reading clubs, and industrial and scientific associations, and now had every invitation to view this and that exhibition, to be registered in most of the institutions as a member, and thus he had something to do from morning to night and saw himself like a big businessman required to divide up his day in order to fulfill the necessary obligations of courtesy, but without limiting himself to much in his own activity.

In order to remain in appropriate contact with Reiner, he had resolved to familiarise him in writing with the story of his current stay. We will thus learn about everything which happened to him in Br. and what experiences and knowledge he collected there from the following letters to his friend.

Dear friend!
I have here through the addresses which I brought with me from my friends there found a good reception; your friend Bonner especially, who expressed a great joy at your letter, concerns himself very much with giving me every encouragement which a stranger in a town unfamiliar to him can expect. The chapter on freemasonry turned up in conversation here straightaway, just as in Hm. and Bl., and he cannot comprehend at all that I am not yet a member of the sublime order. He endeavours to move me to enter, and in order to make the matter quite pleasant to my eyes, he takes me with him to all the gatherings of freemasons where it is allowed. But above all, which I noted previously, he has, despite his understanding and zeal, not yet found the

philosophers' stone, as I have often already heard the essential secret of freemasonry called, and also seems to have no intention of seeking anything else but whatever the story of the day offers him. He has, irregardless of my telling him that I am not free in this respect, not yet stopped reckoning on finally introducing me into the order.

With one such discussion the opportunity was now offered to me to also ask him what the actual goal of the society was. To this question the following conversation arose.

Bonner: "You ask about the goal of the order. I do not comprehend that a man like you should not be aware of it."

Me: "How would that be possible, since the matter is not expressed anywhere, and in every place a different tendency seems to reign."

Bonner: "Unfortunately you cannot yet have been informed about the essential tendency. But that does not take anything away from the matter, since everywhere, be it in this or that branch, you dedicate yourself to the laws of humanity. Seldom does a place offer opportunity to encompass all the goals and produce the proper generality. To bind into a unity all that humanity has in the way of the beautiful, the good, and the sublime, and to produce an all-encompassing morality is the highest and the only true goal of freemasonry."

Me: "You surprise me and give me a view which is so encompassing that the individual must already dispense in advance with ever becoming a complete freemason."

Bonner: "In practise it must admittedly be difficult, but as per the idea, humans are in a position to acquire all the virtues themselves and produce a pure ideal of morality and humanity."

To this I of course did not know what to say, because he meant to portray himself as it were as such an ideal. I thanked him for his instruction and asked him also furthermore not to lose patience with me. He suggested that if I once became a member of the sublime society all would become clear for me. But in order to allow me to take a look in advance into this enormous institution which encloses all the branches of human knowledge and ability in itself, he asked me to accompany him that evening to a gathering where more objects of its effects would be discussed and accounts over them given. I took up the suggestion with polite thanks and promised to present myself at the specified hour at his place.

The evening came. On the way there he said to me that I would meet people from all classes, of whom very many were not freemasons. I walked expectantly by his side and actually found a large gathering in a hall, a bit like in a town hall where those summoned waited until they were called. Bonner obtained for me permission to be led into the freemasons', or better into the gentlemen's chamber.

Now the work began. First someone appeared who desired support for the building of a house ruined by fire and offered to pay it back, but without interest. The wish was granted and the date for paying back established according to extremely cheap rates. Then came a simple townsman whose son was studying medicine at the cost of the lodge on account of excellent talents and model behaviour and needed a number of costly books. The matter was looked into and approved. After this a factory overseer entered who at the inducement of the freemasons kept occupied a number of poor children and had to give an account of whether he had not exceeded the specified hours of work and had kept the little ones entrusted to him from going to school. Thus it continued for about two hours, and you felt urged to say that here more good happened than in any one place in the world.

In eight days there is a large freemasons' celebration in which non-masons can also take part, since it relates to an institution of the lodge which belongs to public life. I will give you news about that and until then will be gathering my thoughts more. I know already in advance what judgement you will make on the reading of this letter. But I will remain silent over that in order to not get ahead of you prematurely. The task which you have set me, nobody here seems to suspect, and hence nothing is to be expected in this respect for us. Farewell! Give my greetings to your friends!

***

Br. —

The celebration is over. I will attempt to give you a small outline of it. Were I a freemason, the matter would be more beautifully described; you must take it into consideration with the layman when he does not describe things he has seen for the first time straightaway with the right colours. So hear!

The day appeared. In the afternoon at three o'clock one entered the banquet hall of the lodge building, which was fashioned for today into a formal lodge, as the members said. At one end of the hall, opposite the entrance, stood a sort of throne with an altar; opposite this were found two smaller altars, each raised a single step, and next to the throne and on the sides of the hall chairs and benches and still more smaller altars.

This arrangement I had the fortune to see beforehand under the escort of Bonner, master of the chair, and at the same time to admire the taste of the master of ceremonies who had put up everywhere it could be done decorations with bunting and symbols of the current celebration. Finally the celebration began. The gathering of non-masons was led in and shown to their assigned places. Then the freemasons entered and sat where they considered it expedient in accordance with the order. So now everybody stood in silent expectation of that which should happen.

Mr Bronner struck with the hammer, his symbol as master, a blow on the altar; two other members, who stood opposite him at the smaller altars, and whom they called wardens, did the same, and with that the celebration was opened.

Bonner spoke with solemn voice, "Humanity!"

The two wardens, one after the other, did the same, and the former continued with, "Humanity is the goal of humans.

Humanity is written in the heart of each one.

Humanity leads us towards our destiny.

For it, that sublime characteristic of human nature, we have today organised a celebration so that we are reminded of it constantly and fulfill the obligations that it places on us. In praise of it I open the current work and ask all those present to support me."

A new blow with the hammer followed. The two wardens repeated it, and the master of the chair commanded those present to hold talks in praise of humanity and to thereby glorify the celebration.

A cantata with beautiful words, beautiful music, and beautiful voices was the first sign of tribute which was offered to humanity, and through which the disposition was transported for the entire celebration into a solemn mood.

There followed now various lectures about the solemnity of the day, of which one distinguished itself especially on account of its shortness and conciseness, and sounded as follows.

"We are celebrating today the founding of an association of the local inhabitants which set as its goal putting limits on misfortune as much as human powers are capable of. At this opportunity it will not be un-fitting to illuminate with a few words the effectiveness and results which have been drawn from that.

The goal of the association which has been around for ten years is charity in the extended meaning of the word. We provide support not only to the beggar on the street or to those who today or tomorrow lack nourish-ment, no, we seek to choke misfortune in its forming and to dispel it by expedient collections and institutions of industry.

The means by which we effect this are the sense of charity and the innate magnanimity of our fellow citi-zens. From all sides contributions are given to us, and even when it concerns being active through calculating and writing, building and collecting, a praiseworthy rivalry arises over who might be contributing the most towards the good.

The results finally are so apparent that every traveller considers our town to be a model for the most various and most expedient arrangements. Institutions for the deaf and dumb and the blind, high schools and trade schools, houses for the poor and disadvantaged, factories and farms have achieved up to now under our eyes and our direction a degree of perfection so that we may joyfully shout out today, on the anniversary of this association, that our task is, so far as it stands within human power, fulfilled, and our fellow men and posterity will yet bless the names of the founders."

The mood of those present was raised by this lecture to a level that many an eye poured out tears of emotion and joy. I myself felt likewise moved by the general urge to set a dam to misfortune, and could do nothing else but consider such a striving to be the worthiest goal of an institution in which the noblest assemble, and which extends over the entire earth.

Yet more lectures were held, alternating with fitting songs, which testified more or less to the details of the effectiveness, but from which at the same time a heartiness wafted which filled every mood with delight and enthused them for ideas of a perfect happiness.

When no new talkers were putting their hands up anymore, a collection was made for the poor. I did not have enough cash on me for the urging of my heart and placed a bill of exchange for a hundred talers, which I had at the time in my wallet, in the box. The sum of the collection amounted to two hundred and forty talers, which was immediately handed in to the administrator of alms. Mr Bonner struck a blow with the hammer, both the wardens repeated it and proclaimed as at the start — humanity. A solemn short prayer, spoken from the altar, closed the affair, and everybody left by and by, filled with emotion and thanks for an institution from which the town and the surrounding area receives so many benefits.

You will ask in what mood I was surely in? In a very happy one, I tell you. The task of controlling misfortune and poverty, of being at hand everywhere with advice and action, and of intervening through the animation and improvement of all means of livelihood in their entirety, is a goal which is able to be worthy enough of occupying an association which numbers the noblest of all classes as its members.

***

Reiner to Gomphardt.

Your letter gave me joy because it taught me that your heart, which had withdrawn too much into itself through a proper, but nonetheless one-sided grief, has again won receptiveness for impressions of joy and for participation in the well-being of others. The idea of dispelling misfortune and of spreading as much happiness as possible is again alive in you, and hence I am convinced that, if the highest end-goal and the highest need of humanity ever becomes entirely clear to you, you will, just like you did at your celebration, pay with valid bills of exchange.

But I am sorry that I am unable to share your views, as if a general improvement and welfare system were the only thing befitting an institution like freemasonry for its exclusive and worthy task. In a German state a high-placed person, without means of state and without freemasonry, led merely by an inner energetic drive, has performed with the help of collected private means all that which delights you so much, and indeed in some respects more expediently. In another town, where there was likewise no freemasonry, an in no way rich, but nonetheless well-to-do man undertook to call to life similar arrangements, and indeed in a way that no corporation could have been credited alone with the merit, but rather that it passed to everyone who contributed through sums, or through administrative activity or private undertaking towards the beautiful and great goal. The Jesuits have been reproached since time immemorial for wanting to have their hands in play everywhere. Look about you unbiasedly in your happy El Dorado for whether you are not seeing something similar with your freemasons. A private man should attempt sometime to enter into competition with them in some branch, and you will learn that it was for them not to do with good itself, but about the honour of having effected it. But I do not want to be hostile; but I cannot condone it when a magnificent institution raises secondary aims to be the main thing and thereby loses time and power for thinking of the actual goal, or, in the case of it not yet being known, of seeking it with manly resolve.

Freemasonry possesses, without that I would though be in a position to unveil it, something positive, something independent, which cannot be exchanged for any other industrial or scientific branch. If you ever decide to enter into the society, this will become clear to you in the first hours! You will irrevocably perceive that only the greatest perversity of the thinking and feeling of the institution could underlie such goals which one becomes aware of in our time with the greatest number of freemasons. Keep your freedom which, once lost, is not so easy to obtain again; your uninhibitedness alone can lead to the truth. Any bias is an entrapment which hinders us from seeing the rising of the light.

My friends and my wife offer their greetings and wish you the best well-being.

***

Gomphardt to Reiner

After I had sent my letter and had thought about what I had written once more unbiasedly, I could have heard your answer in advance. You are right — one forgets through secondary aims far too easily the main thing. You warn me not to fall victim to this mistake, in that the lost freedom is difficult to win back again. I thank you for this hint and will keep it in mind as a guide in all affairs. In addition you have found here a second who is not at all well-disposed to the so-called freemason-humanists and moralists. This one said, when I asked him about his judgement, "Humans like time far too much and would like in order to hold onto it to put monuments everywhere. They think through the lists of names on which they gleam in order to defy through buildings and inventions the ephemeral and to found a lasting existence for themselves. They forget as a result that they already know in sleep nothing more about all these glories, much less in the sleep of death where no dream reminds them anymore of existence either."

This expression stirred my attention, and the following conversation unwound.

Me: "You mean that an essential difference is present between death and sleep in that we still dream in the latter, but in the former in fact no dreams take place anymore."

Him: "According to the testimony of natural views and reason it cannot be any other way."

Me: "According to this claim there would be no more life after death."

Him: "No!"

Me: "You believe accordingly in no persistence after this life?"

Him: "I have not yet expressed my confession of faith. I say only, it portrays it."

Me: "What can yet lie hidden behind this portrayal?"

Him: "Something which must be investigated, won over; a new thing, something withdrawn from the senses, which only announces itself to an accessible, reborn disposition and transports us to where the spirit world enters into the world of the senses and makes visible to us how the here and now and the hereafter are closely connected with each other, indeed are even just one thing."

Me: "The moralist, even if unconscious, aims though at an eternal hereafter."

Him: "But will he reach it?"

Me: "Philosophy makes us into new men in that it accustoms us to live only to the influences of a higher truth."

Him: "The influences of truth are at the mercy of thousands of passages in which its clarity is reduced, often even lost."

Me: "What hope remains under these circumstances for humanity?"

Him: "Have you never given yourself an answer to that?"

Me: "Oh yes."

Him: "And how did it sound?"

Me: "There is no life after death."

My examiner look at me apprehensively after this answer and said, "If I knew that one was permitted to trust you!"

I replied, "Never have I misused the trust of another. Test me! Come visit me as often as you like, and tell me your name and your residence so that I will have the opportunity of seeing you in your household, and then it will be seen whether it is profitable for us to get to know each other better."

He gave me his name, described his residence, and thus the start of a closer acquaintance was made.

I sought to make more detailed enquiries about my strange philosopher and learnt that he was known under the name of Mr Gimper, carried on a pharmacy business, possessed sizeable means, and counted few oddities as pertain to a man of respectable reputation and honour.

The next day Mr Gimper came to visit and behaved with a lot of ease like a man of the world. I alluded several times to the conversation we had conducted the previous day, but he still held back, and did not seem to trust me fully yet. I expressed myself over it; he replied, "Forgive me if I go to work cautiously. I have friends in Bl. They have reported to me about you and your intimate contact with Doctor Reiner who is seeking to prove immortality with the keys of reason, and they prepared me for your acquaintance. I do not know how far you have progressed in Reiner's school; only so much is known to me, that you have not allowed yourself to be led to join the freemasons there."

Gomphardt: "What interest can this refusal arouse in you?"

Gimper: "You have for the object of your entrance made certain conditions which neither Doctor Reiner nor the people there could accept."

Gomphardt: "Which conditions?"

Gimper: "You wanted to know beforehand what free-masonry contained and what its peculiar goal is, the one only applying to it."

Gomphardt: "That is true! That is the condition I have made and will make to anyone who seeks to move me to entry."

Gimper: "And if someone fulfils this condition and reveals for you the particular goal?"

Gomphardt: "Then it must still be allowed to me to examine the goal itself, whether it becomes me and is fitting for my way of thinking."

Gimper: "The second condition is more difficult to fulfill than the first."

Gomphardt: "Why?"

Gimper: "Because you cannot expose an important matter without proper guarantee."

Gomphardt: "What does such a guarantee consist of?"

Gimper: "Of a solemn vow of silence in the case that you do not want to take part in it."

Gomphardt: "Even a reliable friend, for example Doctor Reiner, must not be instructed about it by me?"

Gimper: "Oh he can, but under the same guarantee."

Gomphardt: "Does the matter contain anything that is dangerous for the state, church, and social order?"

Gimper: "Absolutely not. To the extent something of the sort were to be found in it, it would have to be re-vealed anyway by any honourable man because a more recent promise does not nullify the old."

Gomphardt: "Now then I give you my word of honour that I, Doctor Reiner excepted, for whom I vouch though likewise, will observe an inviolable silence over everything which you reveal to me."

Gimper: "This guarantee suffices for me. So listen. There is in Br. yet a second lodge, to which I belong as a member, and which is working on the actual goal of freemasonry."

Gomphardt: "You are making me curious."

Gimper: "It shall bring me joy if I can still your curiosity to our mutual satisfaction. But before I initiate you into our secret, I must ask you to hear my life story, so that you get to know the strange way in which fate has led me to the true knowledge.

I am the son of a linen weaver from R. and developed in the boys' school so much talent that many of our distinguished clientele desired to see me and through praise and small gifts spurred my eagerness to learn still more. One day a gentleman came to our little town and suggested to my father, after he had spoken to me and taken pleasure in me, to leave me to him and entrust me to his care. There were six of us siblings, and you could not hold it against my parents if they did not reject such an opportunity. Left to me was the decision, which, so easy to consider, was to the effect of going away with the foreign gentleman who made such great promises to me. It was all brought into order and also settled to deliver me, in the case that I could not bear the foreign place, free of cost back to my parent's house. The foreigner approved everything, and the next day I went away with him.

We travelled without stop to Paris, where we stayed for ten years, and where my master, who was named Almarkus, Doctor of Philosophy, had me taught in everything which decency and a worldly education demanded. Already after a few years nobody from my home town would have recognised me anymore, so much had instruction and society affected me. My master was pleased by this change and decided to take on a part of my education himself and to develop me into a student of his rare and mysterious knowledge.

Now I learned for the first time what he occupied himself with and from where his wealth, which seemed inexhaustible, flowed. He was in possession of secret means for curing the most difficult illnesses on which the arts and sciences of the most famed doctors failed, and the patients often recovered as if by a miracle. But whether his reputation had not been greater than his skill and whether fortune did not also stand by his side especially, I do not want to investigate now; enough that he was considered to be a man of miracles, and everyone from the highest to the lowest courted his assistance. He showed himself to be a father and benefactor towards me and made the only condition for everything he did for me to reveal to nobody his activity at home and to not undertake anything in this respect without his knowledge.

For hours he had himself locked up with me alone in a sort of vault which was furnished for working, and where he prepared himself the medicines which he used for his cures with his own hand only supported by me as assistant.

At other hours he locked himself alone in another room to which I only later received entry, and studied in old books unknown to anybody. Finally he also gave me permission to look around therein.

My desire for knowledge swallowed them up, and before a year had passed I was in possession of most of his secrets, was in possession of the art of how to become like him a great man, associating with princes and counts, and freeing myself of the ignobility of a dependent life as an assistant.

As much as he could use me, he looked as much with some unease at my skilfulness. One day, when we were making one of the most difficult elixirs, he said, 'I have put myself in your power; only your thankfulness and my trust are the bonds which connect you to me and vouch for your loyalty; all other shackles, and even if they were made with oaths, levity can break.'

I replied with honest disposition, 'My thankfulness is unforgettable, and the trust which you, my noble benefactor, gift to me is the trust of a father to the son which can never be betrayed so long as feelings of love beat in the heart of the man.' — 'On that I am banking,' he said, 'and will continue to let you participate in all

that I do so that you become my assistant, and when I
am no longer, the inheritor of my name and my art.'

Oh, how honest my disposition was at the time! Had
I never disowned it, I would be as happy as mortals can
be. But the serpent of arrogance beguiled me; I betrayed
my benefactor and educator and rewarded his fatherly
trust with ingratitude.

My master was called to a high-placed patient in
Marseille. I waited at his house and read undisturbed in
his books for two days; on the third the butler of Count
Atou came and asked urgently after my master. I said
he had gone on a journey and according to what he had
said would not be back soon. The butler left, but came
back after half an hour. His lord, he said, was lying at
death's door, and he must be helped. If Doctor Almarkus, he continued, is not at home, then might I, who
knew all his secrets, come in his name and undertake
the cure. I certainly to begin with made all possible
objections, but the vanity, my skilfulness too perhaps,
and indeed to test myself on a noble person, on a count,
vanquished all my scruples, and I promised my help on
the condition that my master never learnt anything of
it. The butler assured that not only he, but rather
nobody would be permitted to be informed about it to
the extent that the matter must remain a complete
secret. The reward would fall to me, but the honour
would probably be assigned to the family doctor of the
count.

With the word reward my conscience wanted to stir,
but the count's butler knew how to placate it straightaway again. I promised my help and proceeded, after I
had received a report over the illness, to the laboratory
to prepare the appropriate aids and to take them
straightaway with me. I went to the patient; he was a
worn old man of about sixty years and gave little hope
for a fortunate cure. Only I had gone too far to be able
to turn around again; hence I opened my little bottle,
mixed half a teaspoon full in a glass of water, and had
the patient drink it. To begin with everything seemed to
go well; the patient smiled and said it was becoming

pleasantly warm in his stomach. But soon his face had contorted and he asserted the warmth was becoming too strong and burning like fire. They urged me to help. I had him drink water without drops; but the malady increased. In this emergency a servant of the count had hurried to the family doctor in order to report to him the danger to his lord. The doctor arrived, found him almost struggling with death under the hands of an unfamiliar person on which everybody looked with fearful eyes. "What has happened here", the doctor asked, "that the patient should take such a turn?" Nobody answered. The doctor repeated his question with force. A nurse stepped forth and said, "the count complained about bodily pains, then the butler left, came back with another doctor who offered the count a medicine which put him in this state." — "Who called on you?", the doctor directed at the butler. "The count himself and my concern for his life." — "And who dares", he continued, "to prescribe in this house except me?" — "A famous man," the butler responded, "who has already pulled many patients back from their death, Doctor Almarkus." — "Almarkus!", the doctor cried, "Almarkus! The charlatan, the mixer of poisons! — The entire faculty is against him, the police are tracking him. Where is he, that we can arrest him and prescribe him instead of medicine a jail sentence?" — "Here," a servant said, as he pointed at me. I noted that I had nothing more to prescribe here and fled from there, pushing my way through violently, in order to at least get the books in our quarters to the side. Hardly had this happened than the police entered to seize the good doctor. A police commissioner began an interrogation of me and was very surprised at meeting only the assistant instead of the doctor. He asked where my master was to be found. Since I could not give any definite information, they satisfied themselves with locking up the residence and leading me to the police station.

I spent two days there as a prisoner without having been questioned over the affair of my dealings; from that I concluded that they at least did not assign to the matter the importance which the family doctor of Count Atou suggested, and waited with resignation for the outcome. Finally they remembered me, led me to the inspector of police, who sought mainly to convince himself whether I, despite my denials, was nevertheless not the Doctor Almarkus who was being charged. A police-sergeant who asserted he had often seen my master confirmed my statement. From this I received the information that, if I was in a position to pay the rent for my master and still deposit two hundred franks for any possible complaints, no obstacle would stand in the way of my departure from Paris, only this must take place inside three days.

I thanked him for this information and promised as soon as I arrived home to pay the rent from my means, but to pay the two hundred franks from the proceeds of selling the effects of my master. A police-sergeant received the order to watch over the fulfillment of this promise.

I left my arrest with a feeling which is not to be described. Remorse and a guilty conscience tormented me. The outlook of an uncertain future lay frighteningly before me, and all that I had brought about through levity and vanity after I had shortly before given the solemnest assurances of an unwavering loyalty.

The sergeant accompanied me to my residence, revealed to the house owner the verdict of the police tribunal, who contented himself with it and in possession of the present effects at once vouched for the two hundred franks which had to be deposited. The affair with the police was thus dealt with, and now I went with the entry of the landlord and another neighbour about the production of an inventory in order to expose for sale everything right down to the laboratory equipment. In a locked commode which had to be broken into, we found several precious rings and watches, also a cask which, by its weight perhaps filled with gold, must have been of significant value. I had everything drawn up so that I would be in a position to give an account of everything once I was able to find my master. The furniture I sold to a broker for the sum of eighteen hundred franks, the rest I packed up and I left on the third day the city where fortune had smiled so amiably on me, but which I had trampled on in my unforgivable levity.

My first destination was Marseille, in the hope of meeting my master there, or at least receiving news about his current abode. I could not learn the slightest news anywhere, indeed he seemed to have not been in Marseille at all. I visited other significant cities of France without any success. In order to investigate his abode all the more certainly, as he was a freemason, I had myself taken into that order, but without get any nearer to my goal. I finally decided to take ship to England, but could not obtain the slightest trace of him, neither in London, nor in other large cities.

In order to do everything which stood in my powers, I took ship again, travelled through Spain and Italy, returned again to France, wrote to the landlord in Paris; but his name seemed not to exist at all anymore. A misfortune has happened to him, I now thought, he no longer lives. Despite this thought, which I could not banish anymore, I had never lain a hand on his property; the cask was still locked amongst my gear. A few specifics of his remedies which I made use of provided me for a long time with the necessary upkeep until I would have the most unequivocal evidence of his death in my hands.

To satisfy my urge for knowledge and to foster my education still more, I dedicated myself with all diligence to freemasonry, of which I had received through the talk of my lord a high idea, and hoped to obtain through it strength of spirit in my pressing circumstances. But here my expectations failed me completely. No single positive principle which would have referred to anything, to a similar matter, was expressed. The whole thing revolved around a beautiful, regulated ceremony which you adorned with moral, historical, political, Christian, and anti-Christian sentences which dispensed with any inner meaning. Tired of this playing around I took a ship to Palermo, resolved to linger there a while in order to get on to the trail of the remnants of the old Rosicrucianism, or perhaps even a few secrets of the world-famous freemason Cagliostro.

I came to Palermo and soon had a circle of men about me of whom each glowed with a thirst for higher knowledge closed to the common man. We had set ourselves no less a task than to summon the spirits of the dead in order to have them teach us about them and initiate us in all the mysteries. My wish was at the same time to see my master, to ask him for forgiveness, and to hear his will over the use of his estate.

If the dead still live, I said to myself, then my master must appear, give me testimony of the persistence after death and assure me in an undoubtable way of his forgiveness.

We were extremely active and seemed to be close to the goal; then a few let themselves crave using the sublime art for earthly goals, for treasure seeking, and thus the already visible beams of fulfillment of our wishes flew away, and from a lodge of light it became a playground of the lowest avarice.

This discovery enraged me in such a way that I abolished the gathering, obtained passes for myself, and journeyed uninterruptedly as far as here, where I made the decision to settle down and open my master's cask. Twenty thousand talers in gold were contained in it. Amidst renewed remorse for my actions I vowed to purchase equipment here with this gold, to found a pharmaceutical establishment and to conduct it for the benefit of my unfortunate master or perhaps for his yet to be discovered heirs. My business went well, I lacked nothing but a clear conscience; hence I sought here to continue with what in Palermo I had been disturbed in doing through the base dispositions of my colleagues. Here I am a member of the freemasons' lodge of the n∴d∴ish system in which we assembled in a tight group and exercised practically the art of drawing the spirits of the dead into our circle in order to converse with them. With you, my good sir, I have noticed an aptitude and tendency towards such activity and invite you therefore to connect with us and help to seek through connecting with the residents of the hereafter the highest good of humanity, the proof of immortality."

***

This is the story of Mr Gimper which is important in reference to freemasonry only in that we understand from it that it does not anywhere possess anything positive, and the words which have been put in the mouth of Frederick the Great, "c'est un grand rien" (it is a great nothing) are completely justified. The results which Mr Gimper pretends to have already achieved are indeed of a peculiar nature; but who may believe a dreamer? Were objective revelations of spirits possible, then Amalie would certainly have heard my wishes. Since this did not happen, any objective knowledge of spirits and God is for me a chimera to which I attach no more worth than the colour theory of the blind.

I will not stay here any longer. I must free myself of the freemasons in order not to be led finally also into their great nothing of seeking realities. Were you not a member of the institution, it would have lost all respect in my eyes; but since you still adorn it and find in it workers for your plan, it may remain; only it shall not lead me further into temptation.

Indifferentism, rationalism, materialism, supernaturalism, mysticism, cosmopolitism, politics, and shallow history are the tournament grounds upon which freemasonry roams about, on the other hand not speaking a word about a peculiar content, a particular inner nature because none know it, and thus they pay homage to the grand rien with important demeanours.

This letter has become a book as a result of Gimper's story. Only I had to make you familiar with it in order to inform you of the diversity in which the famed wisdom of the freemasons roams about.

***

Gomphardt to Reiner.

I have left Br. because no goal was holding me back there anymore. I wrote Gimper a note the other day in which I regretted not being able to enter his society in that I saw it necessary to leave Br. I also enclosed in this letter, so that he should not believe himself cut off, a bill of exchange for a hundred talers for the alms account of his lodge. He came the next day to me to thank me in the name of his poor people and to express his regret in not being permitted to add me to his list. "The proof of immortality", he added, "is the goal of your wanderings; with us alone you could have obtained it. Wherever you seek it apart from us, they will offer you beautiful words within which no reality is contained. But it shall not be to know myself connected more closely with you; I must console myself over it the way I had to console myself already over many things. Have a happy journey and think occasionally of me too, a man who came towards you with honest friendship, and will retain this attitude to you until his life's end."

After these words he left me deeply moved. Fate has made him soft and given his character an expression of earnestness which often borders on melancholy. It is a pity that he has become a dreamer and thereby withdrawn himself from human society; you would not only have had to love him, but also respect him. I would give much to be able to tear him from his uncertain state.

Mr Bonner did not want for a long time to believe that I could leave Br. without becoming a member of his lodge. He conducts his system of humanity with the same zeal as Gimper his mysticism. Why can such active men not be shown a path on which they could stroll together as free men and brothers. But such wishes are breathed into the wind and will not be realised until our task is solved and the certain irrevocable proof of persistence after death is found. Will this time ever surely come?

I have meanwhile visited several towns where there are no freemasons, and found absolutely no difference.

The people argue about religious views like the freemasons about their own. The so-called philosophers demonstrate the goal of life with a certainty as though they had themselves solved it in simple arithmetic. Poor associations, art societies, culture, industry and trade associations, death and dumb, blind, and bathing clubs are to be met everywhere as perfectly as if you would have heard the hammer of Mr Bonner, the master of the chair of humanity, in all lands. Humans are in these parts all the same. The rich and noble want to impose their will, the former in order to make themselves important and to attain very large earnings, the latter to free themselves of all worries and, as much as possible, to walk leisurely. Humans are the same everywhere; they strive for everything and possess nothing positive.

Since I could not find anything in the so-called profane world, I have connected with a few clergymen. With whom shall I compare them? With my paternal friend, the Deacon? I have found a few who seem not dissimilar to him; but the others are no hair better or worse than the freemasons. A few remain neutral, like our friend Riccort; others seek in history, like Rinkam; others again are propagandists personified, like Rein-thal, and expect the true spirit of the Christian religion only in the future when humanity has one day matured. There are naturalists and supernaturalists, rationalists and materialists, cosmopolitans and mystics amongst them, as amongst the freemasons; only they seek to clothe everything in a reverent garb. An image of you I have not yet met. You alone have withdrawn yourself from the narrow circle of egotism and dedicated yourself to humanity. The others have only themselves, their petty interests and desires in eye and serve the whole only for their own sake. I cannot stay anywhere for long and feel myself often drawn irresistibly to you or to my home town. From where my next letter will be sent to you, I do not yet know. — Farewell! —

***

After Gomphardt had used the entire winter and part of the spring travelling from one town to another, after he had experienced Lent in Rome and had seen a part of the South of France, he arrived in Germany at Wr. and had already made in the first weeks an acquaintance who drew him in and brought about the decision to linger there and to consider more closely his so often discussed, often admired, and then abandoned again task, and to attempt to get out of it a few points of light. He arranged himself to this end in his guest-house in the most comfortable way, placed his diary again in a writing desk set up specifically for it and resolved that, if he did not find here what he was seeking, he would return to his estate and free himself there in the open air from all that which he had collected in the world only as conditioning and a sort of slave's shackles.

***

Part 3:
The Positive in Freemasonry

Only after long journeying does the earnest seeker succeed
In seeing the goal where the truth is waving to him.

Freemasonry

Gomphardt had not brought with him any special letters of introduction to Wr.; his quarters alone in the best guest-house, the exchange of money at the first bank, even his environs at the table d'hôte soon made him acquaintances, and in a short time he saw himself introduced into some very good company.

In such a way he was invited to an evening gathering at a rich private man's place, at which, the high nobility excepted, a great part of high society had assembled who spent the time with music, play and conversation. Chance had brought him together with a man who with an obliging manner betrayed much understanding and safely gave the correct answer to any question directed at him. He got involved in a conversation with this man over the uses of travelling and revealed, without intending, so much about his own aim in travelling that his conversational partner took an interest in him. They were indeed, when they went to dine, separated from one another, but before they went home, the aforementioned man approached and invited him to continue the acquaintance which they had made that day and to visit him at his house. Gomphardt asked him his name, his house number, and for information on the hours when he could be met undisturbed. The man wrote it down with a pencil on a piece of paper, said goodnight to him, with the wish of seeing him again soon, and left with a party of guests who had connected with him.

Directly on the next day Gomphardt took himself to Mr Rückmann, senior teacher and Professor at the high school. He was amiably received, and when both had taken their seats, the talk turned again to the various goals of travel which you got to know with travellers, and as the Professor developed his views over it with much acumen and judge of character, Gomphardt felt urged to share with him his entire life story, the goal of his journeys, and the experiences which he had already had, right down to the smallest details.

The Professor, who had been listening to him with great attentiveness, said at the end, "Your travel history is the story of an entire lifetime, is actually the story of any human who strives for real knowledge; only one is seldom in the position to properly distinguish the nuances of it and to contemplate them. You know how to separate the principal moments of your life's course so adroitly from one another that I must marvel over it. Only your goal is not yet reached, and it is to be feared whether you will not finally tire of seeking it."

Gomphardt: "I will not tire, in so far as my heart drives me and a solemnly given word obliges me to it."

Professor: "And do you hope to find that which you strive for?"

Gomphardt: "That I do not know. Only I will ask any man of integrity who possesses enough talent to think about such a serious matter to be of assistance to me."

Professor: "And are you not afraid of deceptions ... ?"

Gomphardt: "My friend Reiner has expressed the task too clearly. He desires a proof for immortality which anyone who is capable of thinking to some extent can comprehend."

Professor: "I must confess, you are well equipped. Your friend Reiner, but also your Deacon will remain points of light in your life which will illuminate the way for you in whatever labyrinths you might end up in. Indeed the third, last point, the proof, is still lacking and to the extent you are resolved to follow your task persistently, it shall please me to be able to contribute to helping you obtain this as the goal of your journey, I would like to say as the goal of your life."

The Professor stood up and excused himself for having to break off what had been for him an extremely interesting conversation in order to deal with official business. "Visit me again soon! As often as you want," he said to him as he offered him his hand, and left the house with Gomphardt in order to go to the office of the school administration.

Gomphardt, when he returned to the guesthouse, thought seriously about the last words whereby the Professor had promised him his help, and said to himself, "It would be strange though to find here what freemasons, philosophers, and theologians were not in a position to give me."

He inquired more closely about the character and circumstances of Professor Rückmann and unanimously heard about him only good things, indeed excellent things. He was a man, one person said, to whom great and small turned when there was something to mediate. He was a lay magistrate for almost the entire town, merely through the trust which everybody set in him. He could already have stood much higher, suggested another, if his forthright mind had not hindered him from taking the appropriate steps. He also rarely found time because of sheer work for others to think of himself. Thus sounded the judgement of all who were asked about him.

Gomphardt was embarrassed by this news, out of fear of robbing him of time for more important business, from visiting him again soon. Finally on the fourth day he decided to go to him, and he already had hat and stick in hand when someone knocked on the door, and at the cry of "Come in!" the Professor appeared in order to return the visit and to inquire after the well-being of his traveller. Gomphardt was indeed pleased to see him at his place, but nonetheless rebuked him for having troubled himself with breaking from his many activities. "Visiting good friends", the Professor replied, "is no trouble. We were interrupted recently by the hour hand, and I would like to know though whether you and your friend Reiner could not decide to include a third in your alliance."

Gomphardt: "Such an ally as you could not be anything but extremely welcome to us."

Professor: "Tops! I am joining you and hope you will be satisfied with me. Only I make one condition on my entry."

Gomphardt: "What?"

Professor: "You must become a freemason."

Gomphardt: "You know my reasons for why I am not."

Professor: "These are not sufficient."

Gomphardt: "My conviction hinders me likewise."

Professor: "Then I must be duty bound to remain silent."

Gomphardt: "Forgive me if I have immodestly expressed myself."

Professor: "You do not have to apologise. Every human is free in their views, and I would be to blame if I wanted to do violence to your freedom."

Gomphardt: "My refusal to join the freemasons seems to have affronted you to some extent."

Professor: "If you were to join the freemasons merely through fondness for my person without having any view to obtaining something real and good, you would be very wrong. When we seek a thing, all personality ceases and only the magnificence of the goal may place shackles on us. But also in this we must not renounce the freedom of one's own research in that the errors are so various and at the same time so intertwined. Your friends, the Deacon and Doctor Reiner, are certainly both worthy of our respect, notwithstanding that we must say they are not on the right path. Who can deny another not also setting the same doubt in me, but without altering his favourable opinion of me?"

Gomphardt: "Immortality is the wish and goal of all humans. The belief in it has been lost with me; hence life will possess for me no worth until I have received the thorough proof of it. You appear to be wanting to say to me that it is contained in freemasonry; it must accordingly affront you when I do not believe your words and refuse to join."

Professor: "Then the Deacon and Doctor Reiner must have also been affronted by you."

Gomphardt: "They live for the matter and are raised above any personality."

Professor: "And such a belief, do you think, you must not also attach to me?"

Gomphardt: "I am going astray and making the evil still worse when I strive to defend myself."

Professor: "That is the case if you are not sincere and seek to defend a wrong with false weapons."

Gomphardt: "You are right. I was not sincere towards you and wanted to placate you with excuses. So listen! Not only to the Deacon, but also to myself I gave my word to not join the freemasons until someone told me what freemasonry taught, what it aimed at, and what the aim was that attached only to it. I have heard such various ideas and tendencies that I have become doubtful whether it contains anything independent, and thus I am obliged to remain far from it for so long as until I have obtained the conviction of not plunging into a new chaos."

Professor: "After your experiences caution is praiseworthy, and I would shy from speaking even a word with you about it if your and Reiner's task and my promise to be of assistance to you in solving it did not require me to. So listen then! — The actual final goal of freemasonry is the *knowledge of a prophetic word which lies in all humans*."

Gomphardt: "You surprise me and make me doubtful all anew. The human should be capable of a prophetic word? He should possess the power of connecting himself with the purest powers of an eternal light and breaking through the limits of time? That is indeed the terrible mysticism where the mortal imagines themselves swinging out over his sphere and arming himself with the strength of eternity! — Relieve me of this doubt, then I will renounce fear, and abandon myself to your guidance."

Professor: "Mysticism is just as foreign to our matter as raw materialism."

Gomphardt: "All that the senses perceive which reason cannot grasp is mysticism."

Professor: "Then the harmonious sounding of three notes for a chord is also mysticism, the power of attraction of the magnet likewise, no less the powers of seeing, of hearing, of smelling, and of tasting. Nobody has yet explained how the eye sees, the ear hears, and the olfactory nerves smell."

Gomphardt: "We are supposed to learn to perceive spiritual phenomena which we see, hear, and feel, without our eyes, ears, and nerves of feeling being touched?"

Professor: "That is the usual reproach of one-sided thinkers. Forgive me for using this expression, but I cannot mitigate it. You see, hear, and feel in your sleep while your external organs are closed off. You see, hear, and feel, but in such a way that you are not in doubt over the impressions and can recall them by means of memory quite clearly. Has it ever occurred to anyone to declare the ability to dream to be mysticism? Dreams make us attentive to the capability of an inner perception which withdraws from the critique of reason and, in the free play of life, which acts without our doing anything, sees new phenomena."

Gomphardt: "However, you do not want to see mysticism viewed in that sense."

Professor: "In which then?"

Gomphardt: "The phenomena of mysticism are not images arising from us or in us, but rather are coming from another world in order to give us information about various things."

Professor: "That is the actual mysticism which contends against reason, and against which you must take the field. To the contrary, to awaken the spiritual powers in us, to get to know the eyes which see in dream, those are the fruits of self-knowledge, this is the high philosophy of life, without which we will never arrive at a positive truth."

Gomphardt: "Through this principle, however, we nullify all objectivity."

Professor: "And what is lost through that?"

Gomphardt: "Everything. If there are no spiritual objects outside us, any evidence for the existence of a future life ceases."

Professor: "Who claims that?"

Gomphardt: "I do, the world, the theologians, in part even the philosophers do. Socrates himself had a daemon who taught him wisdom."

Professor: "Everything spoken, written, and explained about this has no objective basis. The spirit of nature and the spirit of God, as it is given to humanity, is an eternal educator which, when we make ourselves capable of understanding it, portrays and educates about everything which happens in it; its word, when we endeavour to perceive it, reveals the un-adulterated doctrine of truth and that wisdom from which the ancients drew and stood as a result as free, regal artists who floated above the transitory and already recognised eternity in the here and now."

Gomphardt: "In this way would freemasonry be a matter which would lie in human nature, and which anyone could learn who took it up?"

Professor: "Should have taken it up."

Gomphardt: "If it were to the benefit of humanity, it would also happen."

Professor: "Already much has been suppressed which would certainly have been beneficial to humanity."

Gomphardt: "But it is not to be denied that some of the confusion and the differences arose from falsely understood doctrine."

Professor: "Quite certainly. But should you therefore not accept a benefit because it could be misused? A priestly caste, so declared an old sage, banned speaking in its sphere because from that strife, calumniation, altercation, dispute, curses, and even blasphemy arises. Did this surely do good?"

Gomphardt: "I must confess, it surely did not do good."

Professor: "Another banned music because it had too powerful an effect on the senses and drew humans into the external world. Did this one perhaps do right?"

Gomphardt: "Certainly not. But here no external good is being spoken of, but rather a different one which could be no good to many."

Professor: "And hence I should not be in possession of any gold because it leads low souls to avarice, to betrayal and high treason. Hence the light of truth should be withdrawn from the masses in order to hinder a villain from abusing them? The sun is for all, likewise so is wisdom. Since positive truth, however, is only to be obtained through our self-knowledge, through the most exact contact with our spiritual nature, it remains a duty to make humanity aware of this almost lost good in order to call up as soon as possible that day where our affair enters into public life and illuminates with its light everyone who comes into this world."

Gomphardt: "This prospect is so beautiful that you would have to be emotionless to not be attracted by it. Show me just one possibility, just one track on which you could obtain such a light."

Professor: "I already before made you aware of the senses by means of which we perceive in dreaming. What sort of senses are they? And from where do the images come which we see there and the voices which we hear there? Can you give me question and answer over it? No, you are as little in a position to as one of the disparaging philosophers of our time is.

Dreams are the first step of a spiritual activity which breaks through the limits of the external world of the senses and creates phenomena for us which lie outside the circle of our usual observations. Indeed you could say dreams lead us to a truth, are of a chaotic nature and no results are to be drawn from them. It is true that they do not teach us anymore and teach us no more than that they are, but open up for the urge of inquiry a new field, as it were a new world where it can collect new experiences. May then these experiences also be yet so imperfect and rhapsodic, we must consider that it is not those, but we who bear the fault because we find ourselves in an extremely imperfect and bound state of sleep.

The second step consists of the ability of dreaming in an awake state. Some indeed wanted to doubt such a capability; only daily experience delivers us proof of it. Those sick with fever do not sleep. Dispositions torn by an idea or a predominant feeling see and hear, according to their opinion with their external senses, the phenomena of the inner life. Whoever here still doubts, make the attempt themselves, endeavour to move the external activity of the senses and the imagination to such a rest that the inner life obtains predominance, and you will obtain the conviction that it never stands still and is always forming, shaping, and speaking. Indeed no consequences for the truth are to be drawn from this yet either, because we are abandoning ourselves still to the play of accident.

The human is free, possesses willpower, and only where this expresses itself can order and truth win over accident. Hence the human should raise himself to the third step and set the task for the images and voices of the waking dream, and say: I want to have clues about this or that. Through such a process he puts himself in that category of his species which can give an account of everything which it sees, hears, and feels."

Gomphardt: "I do not know what to say anymore and thank you for your kind instruction. Allow me to think about what I have heard and to see whether it suits my way of feeling and thinking. What you have told me is so new and unusual to me that I already consider it a duty on account of the importance of the matter to contemplate it and go to work with calm consideration."

Professor: "Tomorrow we will speak more about it. I commend your caution and ask that you reveal to me without inhibition any doubts which could yet stand in your way and to listen to the refutation of them with prudence."

Gomphardt, when he found himself alone, was still full of views which today for the first time were clearly set apart from each other and forced him to the exclamation, "If that which the Professor puts forward is true, then you can rightly say the light illuminates in the darkness and the darkness does not comprehend it. Will I ever learn to comprehend it?", he continued contemplatively. "Will not my own nature takes its revenge for the stubbornness with which I approached it? I will have to illuminate the matter more closely before I make a decision."

In his diary we read about his present crisis in the following way.

The knowledge of a prophetic power in humans is as per the Professor's claim the final goal of freemasonry and at the same time proof for immortality.

Prophetic power — is it present? On what is it based? And under what circumstances can it be expressed? Here the usual power of thought falls silent and the imagination swarms over into a realm where the senses shall make perceptions not only in space, but also in time, perceptions which flow to it from the past and the future.

Reason cannot prove anything here, the attempt must decide, and this you should undertake properly. But if the attempt holds water, if it gives us information about new powers of human nature, then is the proof for immortality given and every doubt vanquished? Prophetic power can be of an individual nature, and then it has delivered for the whole, for humanity, no guarantee.

Doubt has ensnared me, and I am afraid I would not believe the truth if I could feel it with my hands and see it with my eyes. But I am now only what I am, and have therefore also only with myself to struggle.

The next day he went again to the Professor in order to reveal his doubts to him, and to have them vanquished if it were possible. The Professor welcomed him amiably and then asked him how he had slept.

Gomphardt: "I slept little, but thought all the more and for utter thinking found no certainty, but rather only doubt."

Professor: "Let us hear! On what do you still doubt?"

Gomphardt: "Myself to start with, in that the task which you place before my eyes can only be attempted practically."

Professor: "There is no doubt about that."

Gomphardt: "But if it is to be attempted in such a way that the presence of a prophetic power is no longer to be doubted, where then is the guarantee that it can serve as proof of immortality?"

Professor: "In the matter itself."

Gomphardt: "The prophetic power, even if it can only reveal a part of the future, is though not in the position to look through eternity and see our continued existence."

Professor: "That is also not necessary. If it only shows itself to be true for an hour, a day, for weeks or a year, then you may trust it also for eternity."

Gomphardt: "A conclusion on the whole from the detail has no conclusiveness."

Professor: "Here there is no conclusion on the whole from the detail, but rather from smaller circumstances to larger."

Gomphardt: "How do you mean?"

Professor: "The trigonometer who knows the length of a line and the sizes of two angles can measure any distance*, be

---

* [Tr.: i.e. if you want to know how far it is to a church steeple in the distance, you can mark out a line of known length perpendicular to the line to the steeple, and then measure the angles between the perpendicular line and the lines from each end to the steeple. The relationship of the angles to the length of the perpendicular line can then be used to calculate the distance to the steeple. If one of the angles is 90° then you have a right-angled triangle, so the distance to the steeple becomes tan θ × length of the perpendicular line. For example, if the line is 20 metres and the angles 88° and 90°, then the distance is tan 88 × 20 = about 572 metres.]

it one or thousands of millions of feet long. Or do you believe that the distance revokes the correctness of the relationship?"

Gomphardt: "No, trigonometry does not worry about any distance, but rather only about the correctness of the relationships."

Professor: "The prophetic power behaves just the same. The correct relationship of the word awakens it, and it is then all the same whether it activates for hours or for myriads of centuries."

Gomphardt: "My apprehensions are vanquished, and hence I ask you to take care for me of the writing to the Deacon in my name and obtaining for me my release from the word I gave. According to your explanations the matter is of such importance that you must not lose a day in connecting with him."

He left it to the Professor to take the necessary measures for the realisation of his intention and to propose him for the present for entry into the lodge. The Professor asked for the address of the Deacon and promised to do everything which could be profitable and beneficial for this affair.

***

Exchange of Letters

The Professor, a man who, after he had once promised something, did not hesitate for long in carrying out the promise, had on the same day sent a letter off to the Deacon with the following content.

Reverend sir!

You will not be affronted if I turn to you in writing with respect to an odd affair. Your friend and protege, Mr Gomphardt, finds himself in our town and, after learning from me that he would be infallibly able to obtain in the society of freemasons the final goal of his journey, would be inclined to enter this society if a promise which he gave to you in this respect did not hinder him from doing so. Since I can share with you, reverend sir, on my honour the assurance that the statutes of the freemasons' fraternity contain nothing which would be permitted to be disadvantageous to the disposition of Mr Gomphardt, to the contrary, that through this step his confused views will perhaps be ordered and turn into a secure faith, I ask you in his name and for the reassurance of your friend to release him from the word he gave and to give him complete freedom in his actions.

With the assurance etc.

***

Deacon to the Professor.

Your gracious letter has caused me joy in so far as I see from it that Mr Gomphardt knows how to win friends everywhere. But on its main point, giving back his word to not enter the society of freemasons, I cannot relent as long as he holds himself bound by it.

Your honour will, since you are naturally a member and warm adherent of the society, not take my openness the wrong way and see it as an affront when I assure you that I speak from honest friendship for Mr Gomphardt who, despite his bright mind, cannot in respect to religion bear any cause which could distance him still further from it.

I consider the freemasons to be absolutely unsuited to giving religious principles or to reinforcing them. I have in the course of my life gotten to know many freemasons and nowhere found results which could justify the expectations which you set in prospect with respect to Gomphardt. The first sign of a freemason was always that he did not attend church anymore; there you will now not hold it against a clergyman, to whom his profession is sacred, when he considers such a putting aside of Christian observance to be a defect of a sound philosophy of life and would like rather to redress this defect than to extend it.

There can be such natures who are not harmed by hypotheses and bad examples, by contrast their dispositions are strengthened by the sight of perversity; Gomphardt does not belong under this class. With all his uninhibitedness and sharpness of thought, he is though constantly led by his heart, and for such souls child-like belief is more beneficial than hyperbolic conviction. I ask you to examine our friend's character closely, and you will convince yourself that I am right when I do not give him back his word.

***

Professor to the Deacon.

Your letter, irregardless that it did not correspond to my wishes in the main matter, has though made a beneficent impression on me in that I saw from it that love for your friend dictated the words to you. Only since he is not abandoning his plan to become a freemason, and I possess the complete conviction that this step will bring him closer again to the goal which was lost from his sight, I am forced to bother you once more with the written request to release him from his word.

I confess to you that many a freemason is not as he should be; but such also usually only bear the name of freemasons, but are not. They are bearers of the symbols without knowing them and without having the courage and the power to investigate what they have been burdened with. Do you want to damn the matter owing to these unworthies? That you cannot do, since you know that many visit your church without ever have thought about the being and spirit of Christianity. The matter which we are pursuing is sublime and even a testimony to our sacred religion which not only the laity, but every priest should be in a position to give. Since this has confirmed itself for all times and also confirms itself even now, even if to a lesser extent, so you could do nothing else but give every encouragement to your friend so that he can carry out his intention to become a freemason as soon as possible.

To conclude, I will allow myself to add that I am not one of those who are to be turned away so easily. Be prepared therefore, if you have not yet put your objections to the side, to receive as many letters as it takes for one of us two to declare ourself overcome.

***

Deacon to the Professor.

Your last letter is a seeming challenge to a struggle where principles appear against principles, principles which threaten one another, even if not with outright destruction, then with a shifting of the plan of attack, in which I who am not accustomed to such struggles could easily end up in embarrassment. But I trust to the principle of all principles, to the Holy Scripture which will lend me weapons which are not fragile, but rather as firm and strong as God himself.

Since it is mainly about principles, not though about the exercise of them, irregardless that you should recognise from the works the doctrine of an institution, I place my banner against you and ask you: what proof can you bring forward against the truth of the Gospels? To say that it runs against reason — that you cannot comprehend it — means saying nothing. Nobody can comprehend why the wind turns when earth and water are moving in constantly equal direction. If I were not convinced factually by the turning of the wind, I would say: winds are moved air; since the air is a heavy body, it must follow the law of gravity and also as wind remain subject to it.

But the Bible, irregardless of it seeming to the layman to begin with to be somewhat dark, gives us itself a light for learning to comprehend the seemingly incomprehensible, in that it gives us the Holy Spirit which is capable of solving all the puzzles of the Holy Scripture. I ask you to make Mr Gomphardt attentive as often as possible to this doctrine, and if it succeeds in animating the beneficent power of belief in him again, then something has been done for which the eternal will bless you.

***

Professor to the Deacon.

Reverend sir! You are so purely apostolic that I am embarrassed to explain to you my views in respect to the destiny of humanity and to religion.

The human is destined to live. If he does not continue to exist after this life, then as a rational being he has no destiny at all; for to be able to say by means of reason, I have become and will pass away, has no more worth than a breath made into the air which disperses aimlessly. Such ideas darken the outlook of humans and make them attentive to think about themselves and the goal of their existence. Now the view falls on religion and seeks in it satisfaction. Happy are those who find there what they are striving after! They are removed from the storms of wandering and seeking, and walk with the blissful feeling of belief towards the goal. But those whom religion does not satisfy, whom faith cannot draw to itself and animate — where shall they seek? Perhaps in the philosophical systems which have been destroying and oppressing one another for centuries? Or in the philosophy of nature which God, like any other creature, makes arise from the material? Either Bible or freemasonry! One is an indispensable necessity to the human. But the free thinker, the man of purified reason and bold heart must possess both, be Christian and freemason at the same time; then he can place himself opposite the orthodoxy as well as the unbelief and the heresies of the world, and as divine philosopher claim those dignities which the power grants him to enlighten the others as an example of pure humanity.

I ask you to take to heart this view which arises from the nature of the matter and to not resist any longer the wishes of your friend and myself.

***

Deacon to the Professor.

Your last letter almost made me of a different mind and tempted me to the return of the word given to me; only then old experiences which I had had in contact with freemasons passed over me and reinforced the decision anew to not give my consent to the intended step.

I was willing, since you yourself are a freemason and take care of the matter so worthily, to pass over all the censurable things which I know about freemasons and to keep merely to the matter at hand. But since you insist with unflinching persistence on your intentions, I see myself forced to explain openly to you, although it contends with my ways, the causes of my reluctance towards your institution.

In the beginning of my clerical career I heard much spoken about the order of freemasonry and made efforts, partly from texts, partly through acquaintances, to learn something positive about it. In the texts of which, although they are written only for freemasons, you can obtain a number with effort and money, I found a chaos of contradictions which were absolutely not to be united into a whole. Here darker mysticism, there a freedom of thought that you shuddered before. The solidest thing I discovered in historical works, which though did not refer to any tendency, but rather argued over documents, over genuineness or falseness of the transcriptions, and over personal authorities. Of a unity, a higher standpoint, there was no trace to be found anywhere. For this reason I struck the matter out of my mind again and did not think about it again for a long time.

After a few years again several advertisements of freemasonry writings came to my attention, which once more awakened my curiosity; only I resolved, before I got involved in the reading, to make the acquaintance beforehand of a few freemasons in order to better instruct myself through a living interpretation of those writings. But how I saw myself betrayed there! Not even one of them to whom I turned knew how to give me a thorough answer to my question. Indeed all entrenched themselves behind the ban on being permitted to speak; but my suspicion that they knew nothing became for me almost a complete certainty. One of them indeed did not lead me into any lodge, but to a few of their private gatherings and hoped to thereby win me over to their cause. But what I heard there I would rather have never heard. Not even a serious word, not a well-worked sentence was spoken which could have reminded one of them that they were in a society which occupied itself with higher views on life. Improper, in part indecent conversations made up a great part of the discussion, and I had to tell myself every time on going home that I could have heard better things in any other company.

I was resolved to withdraw myself in future from any contact with freemasons, but on account of my position as pastor came into conflict with a few members of the order with whom every time the freemason, and indeed with right, drew the shorter end. I saw freemasons through argumentative tendencies become such bitter enemies like were barely found in the times of the League and the Huguenots*. From these fruits I reached conclusions over the trunk and hence made my friend promise to never enter into this society.

You have undertaken to show me the institution from a better side. I also do not want to doubt that men of your mind could not find something good in it, as in the main the pure everywhere see only the pure; only for our friend Gomphardt, who sooner or later must part from you and be left to the guidance of other members, a society put together from such various elements cannot be suitable because, after the first exaltations have flown by, he would necessarily lapse into an apathy which would put his natural good-naturedness in danger. Hence I ask you again to refrain from your intention and to let Gomphardt wander the path which his heart is leading him on.

***

Professor to the Deacon.

The amicable disposition which you show towards me seems to be supposed to some extent to moderate the hard incriminations with which you burden the freemasons, and I thank you also for this manner of proceeding in that it would be unpleasant for me to know myself misjudged by you. Only your incrimin-ations are not of such importance that I would have to fear teaching you a different opinion. Is there then an

---

*   [Tr.: the French Catholic League and the Huguenots were on opposite sides of the French Wars of Religion (1562–98).]

institution amongst humanity which does not stand on the point of losing its original aim, provided that it has not already lost it? — Good, charitable men pool together money, erect poorhouses and orphanages, and avaricious administrators enrich themselves at the cost of the kind-hearted and of the impoverished. Where humans decide to perform a useful project, others seek to use their naivety and to put themselves at the head of it. If you consider the Christian religion — what a number of non-Christians you will find amidst its adherents! Would you now want on account of these non-Christians to not form one who approached you about it into a Christian? Has this consciousness ever hindered you from baptising a child? If we go further in the investigation of the history of Christianity, you might often think it was present for the corruption of humans; for are there not robbers and murderers amongst them? Christians have prepared for other Christians bloody weddings. Christians depopulated Christian lands during the Thirty Years War, sacrificed old people and children to fire and sword, indeed raged so that the wildest barbarians, even the hyenas would have not have been capable of worse. Who conducts still today despite all state intervention the most shameful trade which hell could not conduct worse, the slave trade? Christians! If such incriminations fell on the members of our institution, you would indeed not have any more right to damn them, than with the Christians, but still some right. But since the errors which you charge the few worthy members of the freemasons' association are only consequences of their levity, of a badly calculated ambition, or even of their ignorance over the aims of the order, then I may brazenly say freemasonry is standing there still as the purest amidst all the institutions of humanity because it has never given the word for blood and murder, never placed itself at the head of inhuman, avaricious speculations, but rather only taught and exercised tolerance, morality, and love of mankind, even if not always in the most perfect measure.

I hope to have refuted all your objections, and look forward to a favourable answer. Indeed I would require, if freemasonry did not make the greatest honesty and sincerity my duty, no further permission from you, because you expressed yourself in your last letter not only negatively, but in a pleading way, and then even encouraged me to let Mr Gomphardt wander the path on which his heart is leading him. His heart is driving him to us, and hence I could relieve myself of your further objections. But in order to give you a proof of my great respect, I will not act to my advantage and will make my further decisions dependent upon your reply.

Deacon to the Professor.

Your defence of freemasonry against Christianity has indeed forced me back into open battle, but in no way vanquished me. I have withdrawn according to all the rules of tactics into my entrenched position where you have to attack me if the desire to fight will not perish at the sight of it. Entrenched you see me, and indeed with weapons against which yours cannot achieve anything. Contemplate at once my means of defence, and then consider whether it will not be better for you to lay down your weapons.

Christianity certainly has many adherents who know nothing of the spirit of it and are also not concerned about the knowledge of it; but it stands in a solidity and strength before us against which the forces of hell are put to shame. I will lead this solidity, this strength in a short time before your soul in order to perhaps keep you from further useless struggle.

Freemasonry, say your adherents, is an institution in which the most glorious symbols are drawn up. The Christian church, I say, is an institution possessing symbols which are no less glorious.

Freemasonry boasts glorious symbols, but makes use of them only as signs of recognition of the members amongst each other. The symbols of the Christian church are so essential that they arise from the matter itself in that the matter could only be described by the given symbols. From this initially invisible difference the worth of the one and the unworthiness of the other is documented.

Symbols as mere signs of recognition have since time immemorial been a peculiarity of all secret societies. These agreed over names, signs, and gestures in order to mutually recognise each other, but chose such objects for symbols which even, in case they were discovered by others, stood in complete opposition to the intentions and the tendencies of the alliance. Symbols were the signs of the society, but not their goal, and thus they could perform all possible good and evil plans under the sign of their symbols. For this reason as well, interdicts were always being enacted against such secret societies which were bound by no law and no symbol to a firm tendency. Look by contrast at the Christian church! In it there is no accident, no deception, and no arbitrary results. The symbols are taken from the real presence of God and from the nature of humanity. Everything may perish, everything may be denied by negating writers — the symbols, grounded in creation and in the innermost being of the human, cannot perish though because, written in the hearts of mortals, they are one with humanity. And freemasonry, this daughter of time, this concealer of itself, which possesses no firm altar, no positive doctrine, no centre, in a word no single essential thing, only its peculiar symbol, wants to enter the lists with an institution like the Christian church, where the accidental things are banished, the lies denounced, wilful interpretations reproached, indeed, where on the altar of eternity the most glorious symbols gleam which call us to life, to death, and to resurrection.

To completely fill in this image, a book would not suffice; enough if I say solidity is better than looseness, strength better than weakness, and agreement better than disharmony. What good can come from an in- stitution in which the symbols do not agree with the tendency, the tendency is not contained in the symbols? Every day can produce new ideas so that you stamp into the dust today a matter for which you had enthused only yesterday. The accidental is eternal anarchy, and no government should tolerate an institution in which firm principles do not reign and unalterable symbols, not to be misjudged, are not raised.

If you could read in my heart how much I despise all ephemera, you would approve my refusal. Nothing is more dangerous for humans than to always pass from one thing to another. Anyone who has a good base should lay the foundation and build on it. Even if then storms and downpours come, his house will stand and offer him shelter and protection in bad weather.

***

Professor to the Deacon.

You have directed from your entrenched position a fire at me that, if I could not rely on the goodness of my matter, I would refrain from any further attack. Only, since just as solid weapons as those you possess are at my disposal, it becomes easy for me to withstand any storm.

You say our matter has no firm altar and no secure symbols. Whoever told you that, and be it a master of the chair, even a grandmaster, they just do not know what freemasonry is. Arbitrary interpretations of the symbols of an institution — that is certainly the most despicable thing which it can encounter. If the tendency, as is unfortunately frequently the case, cannot be completely extracted from the symbols, often even standing in complete opposition to them, then that is a renouncing of all loyalty and honesty, because you seek thereby to fall into lies and to at most erect an altar to cleverness instead of to wisdom. You cannot despise such games any more than I. You cannot feel stronger than I how deeply humanity sinks down when it abandons all the pillars of eternity and makes a sacrifice to the attributes of time. If this evil reigned in freemasonry alone, then you could console yourself to some extent, but since we see it everywhere, that even in the treatment of religious laws homage is rendered to the accidental, often even to the fashionable, no solace remains to us than to not be weary here where we stand and to struggle with all our powers for the solidity of the matter.

I am digressing actually entirely from my theme and getting mixed up in dissertations which indeed are relevant to the matter, but do not especially touch my intentions. Your friend Gomphardt wishes to become a freemason in the hope of ordering his views on life, perhaps concentrating them again. Let him make the attempt! Our institution has the property that you are not bound to it and can leave as soon as you are no longer convinced of finding what you seek. He will learn to get to know new objects, new symbols by which he will perhaps be able to find his inner-being again and obtain belief or conviction regarding immortality.

Immortality is the basis of human life. This basis is lacking for our friend; with the gaining of it, he will realise a new life, and everything about him will attain meaning and faith.

I close this letter with the wish to get to know you personally. You have shown yourself to me through your description of the symbols of Christianity in a light which shines even now in my inner-being. Had we only such clergymen who were in a position to consider Christianity in its unalterable symbols, how glorious it would then have to stand for Christianity! But we are happy if we only see from time to time a solid pillar which bears the building in storms and preserves it from collapse!

Your friend Gomphardt greets you and asks for a friendly answer.

***

Deacon to the Professor.

You have attacked me in my entrenched position with weapons against which I possess no protection. Your friendship and sincerity, your zeal for all that is good, I cannot withstand it any longer and find myself inclined, even if not to surrender, to a capitulation. Since such a thing must also be welcome to you, you will certainly be happy to fulfil the conditions which I am suggesting to this end.

Everything which humans do is by and by infected and profaned by the imperfection of the earthly. I can say nothing more against it and ask only: how can freemasonry give information about immortality when one no longer believes the Bible, when one grants this book, which alone expresses itself over the laws of life and of eternity, no authority? Were freemasonry in a position to achieve something in this respect, then it would have in our times, in which one attacks the gospels in their innermost sanctum, seeks to rob them of their divine origin, in which one in a word drags the Christian religious doctrine down to a common sylla-bus, it would have in these times opposed this current of corruption and shall have defended it against the spread of life-killing doctrines. Instead of this the freemasons speak of humanity, ethics, and morality, but do not exactly set themselves noticeably much ahead of others on these points. Certainly Christians are also not as they should be, and share with it the lot of their institution in that they let themselves be pulled by the current and do not heed their higher calling. And hence not a word more against freemasonry, but rather for the aim of this letter!

I said above that I am resolved to capitulate, but still reserve the right to set conditions. Everyone seeks more or less their advantage. A kindly fate has brought me into contact with you. You can give me information about your institution, which stands so mysteriously and often so strangely before our eyes, and satisfy my desire for knowledge which I have been nourishing for years. On this condition I give back his word to your friend Gomphardt and wish him luck entering under your guidance a life course on which you have gathered such glorious fruits. Our friend's fate lies thus in the present case in your hands, and I doubt all the less in the fulfilment of my condition when I rightly have a compensation for my efforts and care to appeal to. The conditions rest on the answer to the following questions:

1. Has freemasonry a peculiar goal applying only to it alone?

2. On what basic principle does this goal rest?

3. Is the achievement of this goal useful or necessary to humanity?

The questions are short and concise. I ask you to answer them just in just as short and concise a manner. In the assumption that you will not be leading me to the usual playground of the freemasons, where they outdo each other in the praise of humanity, of constitutions and documents, ever according to the measure of their oratorical talents, I give you already in advance the full power to act according to your best insight and thus remain —

***

Professor to the Deacon.

Your letter has given me inner joy and shown me the purity of your disposition as though in a clear mirror.

You want to stand back from the struggle and capitulate. In order to show you that I too can be a magnanimous fighter, I will subject myself to your conditions.

You ask, "Has freemasonry a peculiar goal applying only to it alone?" On this I can answer you with the fullest certainty, "Yes, it has such a goal."

Then you ask, "What is this goal?" To this I answer and, like Alexander with the Gordian knot, I cut the present one and say, "Freemasonry is the belief in a prophetic power in human nature and the possibility of awakening it."

The third question reads, "Is the achievement of this goal of humanity useful or necessary?"

If the knowledge of the most sublime characteristic of human nature is useful, then the answer goes without saying. But if the knowledge of the most excellent characteristics of each thing is necessary for the knowledge of it, then the human must, in order not to abase his nature, recognise the necessity of a prophetic power.

I see in spirit how you will be astonished at these answers, but I cannot take them back. I hear you asking doubtfully, "If it is so, why do you not say it?" You tell it to the world, but the world does not believe it. You tell it to the freemasons, but even though everything which they hear and see is directed to it, most of them do not want to believe it and do not want to comprehend it.

Humans are as they are, incredulous and sensual. They like to speak of important things, but only a few have the courage to perform important things. This shows itself already in common life, all the more in the spiritual where the external enticements are lacking and no other reward is to be had but that which we give to ourselves in consciousness of our sublime destiny.

"Of whom can one expect", you will ask, "belief in a prophetic power, when one does not believe in immortality?" I turn this question around and say, "How can one believe in immortality, when one does not believe in a divine, prophetic power in humans which sees into the future?"

But in order to lead you to the basis of our doctrine, I must tell you that we draw it, just like Christianity, from the Bible, even from the gospels. We accordingly walk on the apostolic path hand in hand with the priesthood and witness factually what they learn from texts. In order to create a clear idea for you here, we will open the Bible at once and read a part of the first chapter of the Gospel of John. There it reads:

1. In the beginning was the Word, and the Word was with God, and the Word was God.

2. The same was in the beginning with God.

3. All things were made by him; and without him was not any thing made that was made.

4. In him was life; and the life was the light of men.

5. And the light shineth in darkness; and the darkness comprehended it not.

6. There was a man sent from God, whose name was John.

7. The same came for a witness, to bear witness of the Light, that all men through him might believe.

8. He was not that Light, but was sent to bear witness of that Light.

9. That was the true Light, which lighteth every man that cometh into the world.

10. He was in the world, and the world was made by him, and the world knew him not.

11. He came unto his own, and his own received him not.

12. But as many as received him, to them gave he power to become the sons of God, even to them that believe on his name.

This is the hieroglyph which shows to Christianity and to freemasonry their particular individual paths to the same goal.

When we consider the sentence construction of the above verses, a mistake shows itself between the tenth and eleventh verse which no schoolboy would allow himself to be guilty of; for there it reads, "He came unto his own and his own received him not", whereas previously it was always the word being spoken of; it should thus instead of "he", be "it"[*].

If in the five first verses it refers to "the word", it cannot in the eleventh be called "he". But if "he" is the proper pronoun, then previously instead of the word "word", "Christ" must be referred to[†]. But whatever explanation it has with this word construction, the intention of the evangelist to write for two institutions is expressed anyway in verses six to nine in the most unambiguous way where it reads:

6. There was a man sent from God, whose name was John.

---

* [Tr.: Luther's Bible has the German for "it" starting verse ten, rather than the "he" of the King James Version. Lines three and four also have the equivalent of "it" where the King James Version has "him". Otherwise they match up.]

† According to the specification of the author, the gospel of the Christians would read as follows: In the beginning was Christ, and Christ was with God, and God was Christ. The same was in the beginning with God, etc. [This note is by the German editor.]

7.   The same came for a witness, to bear witness of the Light, that all men through him might believe.
8.   He was not that Light, but was sent to bear witness of that Light.
9.   That was the true Light, which lighteth every man that cometh into the world.

It cannot be expressed any clearer that here the talk is of a light which all who have lived before Christ, all who do not know his teachings, indeed all who belong to other religions and serve foreign gods, enclose within themselves. Christianity illuminates those who receive its consecration. The light of which John the Baptist gives testimony excludes no human being and is for this reason to be considered as the trunk from which the Christian religion, as divine branch, has sprouted forth.

Can you or anyone, if you examine these verses without prejudice, find another meaning? Impossible! You can at most ask, "What has freemasonry to do with these four verses?"

The essential freemasonry is called St John's masonry. John the Baptist is the patron saint of the order, the members of it are disciples of St John; as such they are called accordingly to continue that which their patron began and to evermore bear witness to the light which illuminates all humans who come into this world.

Now it is to be asked what sort of light it is of which they should bear witness. The answer is, if we examine it impartially, contained in the gospel in that in it a word is spoken which is God, who has made everything which was made, and which is the life and the light of humans. These verses refer to the word in its highest general power and meaning. In Christianity it includes the personified word given for the time and the adherents of its doctrine. Christianity is a product of the word, but the word is the eternal power. Christianity indeed also teaches the word, but through the Holy Spirit and all the Christian virtues; the word, however, in its primal power can only be awakened through itself, through the elements of language in form, tone, and thoughts. The doctrine of Christianity is a divine specific characteristic; the doctrine of the word rests on the primal power and leads us, in that it connects us directly with God, as complete initiates into the temple of Christianity.

From that emerges that to which freemasonry has to bear witness, and what influence it exercises on religion itself. The Christian church is attacked and undermined from all sides, the spiritual foundations are being undercut, its effectiveness denied, the effects of its symbols reduced to folk tales, so that if not one living witness rises and reinforces its truth, it would have to by and by disintegrate and sink down into an heretic mythology.

"But through what means", you will easily ask, "is freemasonry in a position to give such testimony?" The answer is given by the verses of the gospel almost of themselves — through the light of human life which comes from the word that is God. When the human has learned to recognise the light of his life, which has been granted to him by the word that is God, in its innermost power of light, in the word he possesses that prophetic power with which the apostles and prophets announced the truth and the proof of immortality factually.

No light, neither of time, nor of eternity, is in the position of giving a proof for immortality, but alone the prophetic power can. Only this power, even if it is capable of looking just once into the life of the future, can give testimony about the future, about immortality, about the truth of Christian doctrine, as well as the entire Holy Scripture. Without a living testimony the faith in the divinity of any doctrine perishes; without the testimony of a living word the written word turns into waste paper and becomes incapable of maintaining the belief in God.

You can reproach me that I speak here dictatorially without providing proof. It is true. My feelings sweep me along, and I speak as if everybody were just as convinced of the truth of my claims as I am; yet the necessity of a living testimony cannot escape the honest observer when he sees how all indulge only the worldly, all strive only for pleasure and vanity and at most see the forms of religion as a chain in order with which to fortify worldly affairs through ceremonial customs a little more. I invite you yourself to bear witness to this, and you will not be in a position to deny it.

I have written much and see that I will be tiring you; only the topic is so important, so inexhaustible, that language almost does not suffice to say only the most necessary. Seek to order the matter a little with your uninhibitedness and your acumen, and I am convinced that you will consider our institution with more favourable eyes and wish your friend the same fortune on his entry.

Finally I must add that frequently the learning of the whole leads to the knowledge of the particular. Thus it will and must occur with Gomphardt. The religion as a species has lost its effect on him, and so nothing remains but to lead him into the sea of all knowledge from where he may then investigate the outlets of the rivers and streams.

***

Deacon to the Professor.

You have not only shown me in your letter the principles of a philosophy that is new to me, but of a theology. Your interpretation of the introduction to the Gospel of John is so new and surprising that one must think for a long time about whether one has also read it properly. With repeated examination, however, the matter seems so natural that one thinks that not you, but rather our own understanding has given us this interpretation.

Your views on Christianity and freemasonry give me so much to think about that, since I have come into contact with you, I have set all other philosophical studies to the side. You have unveiled the foundations of a positive and living philosophy and theology, and since then I have not wanted to enjoy any learned book anymore. But one thing I carry in my heart which I do not know how to explain and which unsettles me to some extent. You must have noted from my earlier letters surely that all doctrines which do not emerge from apostolic principles do not find any entry or any belief with me. Now I know, however, that freemasonry is not expressly connected to Christianity, but rather is practised by Turks, Brahmans, Buddhists, and the adherents of other confessions. Of what now does a Turk or Chinaman, if he is a freemason, have to give testimony?

According to the gospel, John the Baptist, the patron saint of freemasonry, prepares the path for the lord, that is, for the messiah. For whom does the Buddhist or adherents of other religions prepare it? I must confess I feel too weak to untie this knot, and if you had not already given me so much proof of your deep spirit of investigation, I would have no hope of ever being enlightened over this scruple.

Forgive me that I am becoming intrusive; only you have opened the treasure chamber for me once, and I will take from it as much as I can bear, and as much as you are inclined to give me.

***

Professor to the Deacon.

The question which you have given me is of great importance and even in the halls of freemasons it is not yet explained fully everywhere. Freemasonry, which works on a light which illuminates all humans who come into this world, must thus also be able to illuminate the Turks and Moors, the Brahmans and Chinese, in short all peoples who do not hide themselves from it. Now it is to be asked what then the testimony that they have to give refers to. Where there is no written word, no testimony about it can of course take place either, and the living word which freemasonry is seeking to awaken then mainly deals with itself in order to testify to the divine in human nature. Furthermore every nation possesses though, even if not in writing, traditions which refer to a divine origin for their ancestors and to spiritual actions which can be examined, purified, and recognised in no other way than through a living word.

In the primal state humans still had no writings; the voice of the inner spirit alone, that Christ residing in all humans, even if you did not know his gospels, was then the guiding principle and doctrine for life and had to work, the less they were intimidated by instruction, all the more freely and unhindered. But I must here state another question in your name and seek to answer it.

Many claim freemasonry has become dispensable through Christianity. In certain respects it may be; though, as already mentioned above, Christianity needs a constant living testimony in order to protect it against the attacks of high-spirited book learning and to confirm its value. But this is not the only basis for the necessity of freemasonry; this lies still much deeper.

Christianity seeks the same living word freemasonry does, but with other means more suited for the great masses, namely through the awakening of the Holy Spirit. Freemasonry goes on a straight path to the goal, combines with visible and invisible means the creation with the power of the creator and gains thereby the science, the free knowledge, whereas the former is ever active in a realm of grace and considers the obtaining of it always as a gift, not as something self acquired.

I foresee that this sentence will be a little opposed to your apostolic views. But if you look around unbiasedly in the Bible, you will find in the teachings of Christ and his apostles, but particularly in the Book of Wisdom* and in the Psalms of David, clear hints of such a freedom.

In the beginning there was no school; everyone learned through illumination by God. Sins made school necessary in order to show their adherents the way again of achieving life with the pure.

---

* [Tr.: The Book of Wisdom, or the Wisdom of Solomon, is included in the Cath-olic canon, but is not part of the King James Version of the Bible.]

Johann Baptist Krebs

***

Gomphardt as Freemason

G omphardt had meanwhile become a freemason and was striving to get the true interpretation from the symbols. He spent three years before he arrived at complete certainty. After he felt, however, the first radiance of the light of them, he surged from step to step until he could write with complete certainty to the Deacon, "There is a life after death; I have found the irrefutable proof of it and rejoice again in life like a youth who goes to meet the most beautiful prospects of his existence."

He also wrote to his friend Reiner and summoned him to visit the lodge diligently, to consider the symbols there, and to examine their interpretation there, but not historically or through rational logic, rather *practically*. Reiner followed his advice, had instruction given by him, and obtained through practice what he could not have obtained through all the deductions of reason.

The Deacon undertook a constant exchange of letters with the Professor and, since he had learned through Gomphardt of such glorious results, expressed the wish, if he was not too old, to himself become a freemason. The Professor wrote to him in reply, "As high as I place freemasonry amongst all the institutions of human society, I cannot advise you though to carry out your wish. The highest goal which humans can achieve has been granted to you through a living apostolic belief and through the spirit of Christ. The means by which freemasonry leads its followers would indeed not suppress what you possess, but also not elevate it. Remain on that path on which you have wandered so safely up to now, and thus, as we have found ourselves here, we will also find each other again there."

Gomphardt told often about his journeys, spoke each time with a few regrets about Mr Gimper and wished yearningly to give him news about his teacher and to be able to reconcile him with him. The Professor, who as the inspector for a mineralogical office had correspondents in all the significant cities of Europe, finally invited each of them to enquire after a certain Doctor Almarkus and, in the event that they learned something, to provide news about him in the next despatch to his address. After about a year he received a letter from Lyon with the news that Doctor Almarkus had been resident there for some time and had acquired through several fortunate cures money and respect.

Gomphardt undertook to write to him himself, to make him familiar with the fate of his former student and assistant, and to invite him to forgive the latter for his error and to make an amicable arrangement over the means which the latter indeed possessed in an unlawful way. With the return post came the answer of the Doctor that he had already long since forgiven his student and had never thought of having the slightest restored. Mr Gomphardt might consider it for the present as a document of his will until the opportunity arrived, which would not be a distant prospect, of negotiating everything verbally. At the close of the letter it read: "In four weeks I am leaving Lyon in order to see the most significant cities of Germany and then to remain for a longer time in Vienna. On this journey I will pass through Wr. and will have myself instructed by you on how and where I can meet Gimper."

The Professor had long since already intended to take a trip to northern Germany and was resolved to carry out his intention that summer at the time of the holidays. Gomphardt himself after five years absence felt like seeing his estate and the Deacon again and going along with the Professor as his companion. So it came about that they were waiting directly on the arrival of Doctor Almarkus and could then start their journey.

Gomphardt had already written to his friend Reiner a few weeks before and insisted on inviting him to visit him at his estate around the 1st October in order to be able to discuss with him there everything he had seen and heard up to then. Likewise he also sent an invitation to Gimper with the request to come there because he had discovered things which were of the greatest importance for him.

The time passed quickly amidst preparations and plans, and four weeks later one evening as Gomphardt and the Professor had come together, Doctor Almarkus gave notice of a visit if it were possible that day. The acceptance was immediately given, and after quarter of an hour he entered the room.

The two friends received him with obliging politeness. He showed himself on first entering to be a man of worldly education who knew straightaway how to find the right note. When the first greetings were over, he inquired after Gimper. Gomphardt told him in condensed outline his story and thanked him in advance in his and Gimper's names for the magnanimous handing over of the means secured in an improper way. Almarkus saw this as a sort of duty in that he had promised to look after him. "The rascal", he said, "seems to have learnt something from me and been blinded by ambition. But I owe to his incautiousness a steadier direction to my career. I was in Marseille and learnt through one of my friends of Gimper's unsuccessful attempt at a cure and the outrage of the doctor. Hence I distanced myself from France, shipped over to England, had myself enrolled at Oxford as candidatus medicinae* and put on the doctor's hat a year later. Now I had a diploma for my medical practice in my hands and began a new career in London with such fortune that I saw myself in a short time as the doctor to the richest houses and even as court doctor. Money, honour, and a glorious prospect were in my entourage; only it went against my nature to constantly linger in one place and fiddle about like a Philistine in the snail's pace of a medical practice where you must make visits for a sniffle here, there an upset stomach, or because of other trifles, twice or three times a

---

*   [Tr.: medical student.]

day, often even at night. Hence I left London, sojourned in all the big cities of England for a time, even returned to Paris, then to Rome and Naples, and returned to France at the express request of a rich banker in Lyon, and now find myself here in order to exercise my art also in Germany." The Professor suggested the current medical authorities could perhaps though find cause to place obstacles in his path. He answered, "With money, skilfulness, and will*, you get by everywhere."

The assuredness of such a behaviour impressed the two friends, and the Professor expressed his embarrassment at being able to be somehow of service, since the Doctor would know through his worldly experience himself how to obtain the most pleasant amusements. Almarkus replied, "I thank you for your kind comments, but nevertheless with the request to make use of being permitted to visit you sometimes as long as I am staying here." The Professor reckoned this to be an honour, and they parted with the promise to see each other again the next day.

***

After the acquaintanceship was made through the appropriate return visits, Almarkus invited the two friends, in order to get to know them better, to an evening meal in a hotel. When after the simple meal Almarkus drank to the health of his friends with a glass of Johannisberg, he recognised them by their response to be freemasons and said, "Now I am doubly pleased by your acquaintance. In this way I can speak without reservation about much which I would otherwise have had to keep silent about or explain with great beating about the bush."

Gomphardt: "You are then truly a freemason?"

Almarkus: "I hope so, and indeed one of those who do not take the form to be the essence like dark monks, but rather who seek the spirit in the form and recognise from this the necessity of the form."

---

*   [Tr.: the word "will" [Wille] has been substituted here for the word "world" [Welt] found in the text.]

Professor: "You express the matter so concisely that I am astonished and ask you whether such sentences are understood in other places and other lands."

Almarkus: "Oh yes, but only by individuals, never by an entire lodge."

Gomphardt: "And yet they exist?"

Almarkus: "As well as it goes. They hold lectures about brotherly love and humanity, argue about documents and constitutions, and call that working."

Professor: "Why, I have often asked myself, was our matter comprehended almost in all ages, and today it is as if you were speaking at walls which, firmly nailed, do not let any sound through anymore."

Almarkus: "That can, according to our way of conducting the matter, not be any other way. Formerly there were men who dedicated themselves to it, now you actually see nothing but observers. In all arts we see three classes of participants — artists, dilettantes, and lovers. Artists are those who dedicate themselves to an art, study its laws, practise its technique, and deliver in this way works of art. You call dilettantes those who alongside other business dedicate themselves to an art, sometimes, if the talent is excellent, quite well, but mostly they deliver extremely mediocre work. Lovers of art finally are the countless viewers who seldom have an innate unbiased judgement and assess the art phenomena according to quickly received impressions, now and then supported on the authority of some critic or highly placed art connoisseur.

Freemasonry is an art and must, in order to develop itself fully, necessarily express its efficacy in these three classes. Now I ask you, which of the described classes make themselves noticeable? Answer: almost none, at most the lovers who would like to have something to criticise and, since they find nothing, place themselves above the artists and damn and deny the artists and art."

The Professor and Gomphardt had listened to this description with rising interest. And when Almarkus made a small pause, the Professor said with a sort of wistfulness, "You are illuminating the matter from a side which I have never seen before; but truly directly from this point of view the history not only of freemasonry, but also of humanity shows itself in a way that we notice the lack of artists in all branches and see only lovers who, because one offers them nothing more, despair of divine artistry and artistic power."

Almarkus responded, "So it is! Not the lack of investment, of love, but rather the lack of artists has plunged the world into a chaos from which it is only to be rescued again by consummate artists. Certainly there is yet little hope present for such an epoch of art, because nobody wants to decide to dedicate themselves exclusively to the matter. And yet without this devotion no result is possible for our institution.

Freemasonry must have artists, dilettantes, and lovers of art as good as any other art. The artists form the forum, form their own class in the chain of the whole. Dilettantes connect to them, and the lovers assemble around them as around an altar, and give the proof that all humans are capable of being affected by the highest productions of art. Artists, dilettantes, and lovers comprise the whole and in this view every art is a common good of all of humanity.

Freemasonry must have artists; then it will be able to place itself again in the rank and file with other arts and sciences. Then it will not need to conceal itself anymore in order to hide its weakness. The artist who still sees too much lacking in his works hides them from the eyes of the viewer; but as soon as he then recognises some perfection, he opens the long closed door and gives his work at first to friends and neighbours and finally to the whole world to see."

Here a pause occurred again; the Professor used it and said, "What our dear brother has said is so true that you feel yourself momentarily convinced. But how is the evil to be remedied in a time like our own in which everybody, bound to their office, their business, and their profession, never wins so much time to dedicate themselves to a matter which grants them neither nourishment, nor outward recognition? The true artist must devote himself entirely to his art, otherwise he does not lift himself above dilettantism. Since now this cannot happen, we possess no hope of seeing freemasonry ever placed so highly as to be able to compete with other arts."

Almarkus: "This is certainly the great hindrance which stands in the way of the emancipation of freemasonry. Only such a thing does not lie in the matter itself, but rather in the lack of energy with which it is treated. We see in all subjects, even often without prospect of reward, men placing themselves at the head of a matter and working on it with a persistence and sacrifice which astonishes us. What sacrifices have been made in the fields of astronomy, of mechanics, of mathematics, and of the other philosophical sciences! Why should the same not occur in an art which occupies itself with the most sacred affairs of humans and leads them to that goal for which they are destined?"

Professor: "You are right, the human can make great sacrifices, but always though with a hidden outlook for external advantages. But here there is also not the slightest hope for it."

Almarkus: "Who says that? Do we know how high our art could rise in the esteem of the government, indeed of all of humanity, if it were conducted again as it should be? It is an art which encloses everything in itself and gifts to everyone who practises it contentment and rest, without which no other good has any worth."

Professor: "It is true. And yet I cannot suppress my sadness, because you will not be in a position to show me amongst all the links in the chain of the society only one who would have dedicated themselves to its goal entirely and solely."

Almarkus: "You, dear brother, have done much, and our friend Gomphardt seems to have made the learning of our art the sole study of his life. Thereby your objections are already factually refuted. But your objection is still less when you consider that any human chooses next to his normal profession a favourite activity for which he sacrifices his best powers and often achieves extraordinary things because he works here with love and his entire soul. The way many a clergyman next to his office of preacher carries on agriculture with a circumspection that places him in this subject amongst the leaders in the land. Just like that I have gotten to know clergymen as virtuosos in gardening, painting, poetry, or music. Many an official shines next to his sphere of his action as a mineralogist, as a mathematician, or as a writer in a quite different subject to that demanded by his office. If the freemasons employed the time which they dedicate to such side-studies to their art, truly they would see greater success, and the institution would not have need to argue about ephemera; it would stand there independently and sublime for the honour of the association and for the welfare of humanity."

Amidst such discussions the time of parting neared. The Professor grasped his glass once more and with it toasted Doctor Almarkus with the following words:

"Thanks to the fate which led you to us.
Your views are lights which should never go out.
May the creator who leads everything to the good spread these lights and open the eyes of the world so that they are comprehended."

"Amen", Almarkus responded. "What I am capable of shall happen, and since I have found in both of you two capable pillars, I take hope again that one day a permanent day will rise amongst the children of humanity."

They parted amidst assurances of steadfast loyalty and devotion towards one another and to freemasonry.

**

One day several brother freemasons assembled, amongst whom Gomphardt, the Professor, and Almarkus were found, for an evening gathering. After they had conversed over the usual news of the day for some time, the talk turned to freemasonry, over which the Professor made the comments thus, "Freemasonry is an institution which has such deep roots in human nature that you must often wonder why it is still hidden from the masses. Everybody who does not enter the path through prejudices and self-made laws of its effectiveness has traces of it which he may only follow in order to come to the most complete certainty of his destiny. All secret wishes and urges are outflows from it, the suspicion of an eternal judge is its source and the need to believe in an extrasensory life is the spur which should drive us; but there we let ourselves be fobbed off with what is given, we do not investigate the source which flows in us and thereby distance

184

ourselves ever further from the goal which we have to reach. From where, I often ask, do all these contradictions amongst humans come, since they go to work in other affairs with cleverness, understanding, and reason, with certainty, solidity, indeed often with a determination that you would believe they were called through themselves to a sort of infallibility which must lead them in all affairs to truth?"

Almarkus replied to these questions, "Those are the sighs which have been heard for as long as the world exists and will be heard while it still exists. The outer nature is too mighty to be able to withdraw from and look into the inner nature without firm willpower. The human who knows how to help himself everywhere thinks for true knowledge of the spirit he must look through eternity and encompass God in his omnipotence; but he forgets that in smaller affairs, in order to learn to recognise them, he must proceed with a reduced yardstick that agrees with his power of imagination. The geometer draws up the recorded area on a small piece of paper, just as the commander draws up the plan of battle. For the portrayal of the earth a small globe serves us, and the astronomer measures the infinite space of the heavens on a chart which is carried in a coat pocket. Should what happens here not also be usable, even necessary in the realm of the spirit? — Thanks be to our fathers, they have set the powers of the spirit, filled by the universe, in agreement with our nature and drawn them up in measured relationships in the lodge, from where we infer the whole and are in a position to recognise it in its infiniteness like the astronomer does the heavens. Only the obstinacy, the arrogance of the human bristles against everything which he has not approved of himself previously, even if not understood by him. But here no approval precedes us, to the contrary only opposition. The clergy has lost the freedom to think about spiritual affairs other than dogmatically, whilst the scholars from aversion to dogma deny away any free spiritual efficacy in advance. For this reason I have in my life spread more light amongst the non-masons than amongst freemasons. Yes, I call upon you, there where you find hearts inclined to higher truths, be it the rich or the poor, be it farmers or lords, be it women or men, make the attempt to show them by means of the symbols of their religion into their inner-being, and you will see how receptive human nature is in general for spiritual activity. We can have an effect anywhere, with the Jews with Jewish symbols, with the Turks with Turkish symbols, with the Christians with Christian symbols, which all point to nothing else but to the awakening of the spirit, to a rebirth in the spirit. But we must be active and not despair, even if there are thousands of obstacles standing in our way; through despair we break the vow which we have given the order, and may in this respect alone abandon the hope of a reward."

All were enthused by this talk and gave the speaker a triple hooray amidst celebratory jubilation.

***

Almarkus had in Wr. visited all the healing institutions and natural history offices, had been drawn into consultation on a few important cases of illness, and behaved everywhere as a man of solid experience, of modest confidence, and with a courteousness which opened all hearts and doors. Many significant men, however, did not have opportunity to come into contact with him, and wished though to make his personal acquaintance. For this reason, a celebratory lunch was instituted, to which he was invited as guest of honour. A great part of the freemasons and a still greater number of the non-masons had gathered so that you saw together at a table positioned in a horseshoe seventy and more of the most educated men of the town.

Towards the end of the meal toasts were raised to the Doctor, all of which he responded to with good manners, often with whimsy. One drank to the much-travelled; another to the highly experienced; a third to the philosopher and philanthropist. A freemason finally raised his glass and said, "To the freemason!" A non-mason then responded, "There we cannot drink with you." — "Why not?", the speaker asked. "Because we do not know what freemasonry is," was the answer he received. Another spoke, "The Doctor should give us a concept of the matter in a short lecture; then we will also celebrate the proposed toast." All those present agreed to this desire, and Doctor Almarkus began.

"Freemasonry is a school in which the basic symbols of all knowledge are established as doctrine. They contain the

186

elementary lines of an eternal and living geometry, and just as we make ourselves through thorough knowledge of the usual geometry capable of recognising all surface relationships, so too do we obtain through the knowledge of of the symbols of freemasonry the ability to resolve the symbols of all peoples and religions.

There are indeed a number of symbols which owe their origin to accident, to the memory of persons and actions, to specific customs and festivities, but often also to no less important events, and hence they possess no generality. Here you can rightly ask: how is a geometric basis to be given by them?

It is this point which led to the Babylonian confusion. Arbitrary signs or allusions are not symbols which lead to a positive knowledge and could be treated scientifically, but rather mere hints which are to be solved like a puzzle, but are mostly not comprehended without special explanation. As long as you count the symbols of freemasonry under this class, freemasonry is also a Babylon where you do not understand each other, and even if you were to be assisted by a thousand histories, a thousand documents, and a thousand constitutions. Since the symbols of freemasonry, however, rest on no arbitrariness, no accident, and no arrangement, but rather are based on the creation, on the characteristics of God and of humans, and are original and eternal, we must consider them, like the lines in geometry, the scales in music, the regularities of the number system, as keys and archetypes by means of which we learn to understand all the symbolic intimations."

The one who had given cause for this lecture expressed his thanks aloud, and all agreed joyfully in the toast: "To the freemason Almarkus!"

After the conclusion of the lunch, seven of those present, utterly excellent men, announced their interest in entry to the association and assembled to this end around the Doctor. The latter said, "What you have heard are the principles of freemasonry. Do not ever let them out of your sight once you are freemasons. Do not ever let yourself be seduced by one-sided tendencies over humanity, morality, and through moral talk. Only the one who has investigated thoroughly the symbols in their essence is purely human, wise, good, and a genuine citizen of the world."

They applauded this, and with the consciousness of having spent the day well not only bodily, but also spiritually, they parted.

***

Gomphardt, who had made a closer acquaintance with a few country clergy of the surrounding area and had received from them an invitation to a lunch with the Deacon Halbring, went the next day to Doctor Almarkus with the request that he accompany him. The latter accepted the offer, and so they travelled the next day in beautiful weather to the village of Gr., two hours distant from Wr. There five clergymen were present themselves and rejoiced at meeting their friend Gomphardt with yet another guest.

They sat at the table, spoke about this and that and finally also about freemasonry. The clergymen, who knew Gomphardt was a freemason, seemed to have resolved to put him in a little embarrassment over this subject. When they went ever further, Gomphardt believed himself not permitted to let such things pass any longer, and said it seemed strange to him to hear clergymen censure an institution which contained the actual and true theology, an institution which anyone who stood at the head of a church should know thoroughly.

They all now declared themselves against Gomphardt who, as Almarkus still remained silent, had little hope of holding them in check. One claimed freemasonry was an institution which had left the Christian church and had founded more mischief in the world than any other institution. Gomphardt denied this, and said, "If one institution has arisen from another, then freemasonry is the mother of all other spiritual and religious institutions." They demanded proof. He gave it as well as he could. But when another called up the Prince Edwin* constitution, which he assured that he had read, and cited the place in which it is said: "And God taught Adam to

---

*   [Tr.: Edwin is the supposed son (unknown to other historical sources) of King Athelstan of England, and supposedly chaired the first grand assembly of English masons at York according to James Anderson's 'constitutions' of 1723 and 1738.]

write," and declared this phrase to be the greatest nonsense, Gomphardt did not know what to say anymore; he turned to his friend Almarkus with the request to support him in his struggle against such fearsome opponents.

Everyone looked up when they saw in their table companion a second freemason, and indeed such a one who seemed firmly saddled against attacks from actual laypersons. The above clergyman repeated once more the phrase with the teaching of writing and suggested, if all was to be defended, for this claim a rational cause would never be found.

Almarkus entered the conversation and began by apologising for entering in a strange house into a struggle which was of such serious nature, and remarked that he could not clear the field until someone awarded him the victory.

"The reverend pastor," he continued, "who challenged my friend Gomphardt, whose ally I have now become, to battle, has touched a point of the culture studies of the brother Karl Christian Friedrich Krause* which has already caused some confusion. — Krause has through the publishing of masonic symbols, but without giving a guide to the unveiling of them, though with the best will to be of use, harmed freemasonry more than all the bad freemasons together. There is nothing more dangerous for the human than to see things drawn up which are entirely contrary to his way of thinking or his manner of investigation. This we also see confirmed with Christianity in particular in our days, where you deny the whole because you are too weak to comprehend a few striking phenomena and facts. You will make allowance for this introduction of mine because an important matter, in order to evaluate it properly, must also be prepared appropriately.

I have one other point to explain before I get to the matter, and that is my promise not to become a betrayer of the secrets of freemasonry! — Had Friedrich Krause only written for freemasons and not let his works appear in the public book trade, then I would not lose a word over the cited point, but I feel obligated to frankly speak my best both for freemasonry and for humanity everywhere this subject is touched. And

---

*   [Tr.: Krause (1781–1832) was a German philosopher and freemason who published two books on freemasonry and in his philosophy saw God as an essence which contains the universe within itself.]

now I ask the honoured company to gift me a few moments of their well-disposed attention.

In the York constitution of the freemasons, drafted by Prince Edwin, it reads, when he talks of Adam, literally thus:

and there God himself taught him writing —

This sentence can be interpreted neither through the preceding, nor through the following in any other way than that which the words express, in that they describe an action which is absolutely not to be named in any other way. Here it concerns a formal instruction in writing which Adam received from God himself. Considered with the usual powers of understanding, this is now a matter which borders on impossibility and as a complete nonsense deserves no consideration at all. It is mostly dealt with in such a way, and taking this seeming falsity as a starting point, you were easily brought to seeing the entire constitution as a work without truth or meaning.

God taught Adam writing — this is incomprehensible to us. We must accordingly see whether God did not teach humans yet other things which are just as essential as the art of writing. The human distinguishes the colours; who teaches or who has taught him that? He distinguishes tones, numbers, lines, and many things of which you should believe you could not have learned this without the instruction of humans. God is in the human and the human in God. Through that the knowledge of all things are placed in the human's soul and in this way directly taught by God. I do not believe that here an objection can be made, and now pass on to the teaching of writing."

One of those present used the small pause and said, "Up to here the discussion was very good; but now comes the knot whose untying I consider to be impossible without the sword of Alexander."

Almarkus replied to this, "And nevertheless the matter is so simple and natural that those who have carried the conviction of it for only a year can barely comprehend why all humans do not also know it without instruction. — But to the matter!

God taught Adam writing. — That cannot mean anything but — God taught Adam to draw letters. — In what way did God perform this instruction? He placed the primitive forms of the letters in the soul of the human, like the colours, musical scales, numbers, and lines."

Here Almarkus made a pause as if his lecture were at an end. The clergymen looked at one another in silence and surprise. Finally one of them turned to the speaker and said, "We do not understand that."

"And yet exactly that which I just said is the the basic principle of nature, of its movement, of its activity — is not only the spirit of life, but life itself, is the light which comes from God and is God, in a word that philosophy of humanity by means of which it can raise itself to God, unite with him, and become one with him. How poor would humans be if no harmony, no melody, no numbers lay in them. How rich though are they when they have investigated and practised the elements in all the branches of art, and thereby raised themselves to freedom, to independence. Language — what does it consist of? Of words. Of what do these consist? Of letters. The letters are the elements of all languages which are, were, and will be. The letters are unalterable, their composition is infinite. The unalterability of the letters has, however, become an hypothesis, and even if you concede unalterability to them after the pronunciation and the effect which they make on the ears, the characters have for the eye, the actual art of writing, become entirely the play of accident. The letters, namely the vowels, have their form based in nature which we learn to feel with a bit of attention as clearly as we distinguish the scales of music. The plan of creation, the model of all that has become, and at the same time the word of wisdom which gives us natural information about the seeming puzzle of life is contained in these primitive forms. To place before our eyes the primitive forms of the letters was the main business of all the wise ones of antiquity, is also the key to the unveiling of all the hieroglyphs of the Egyptians, mages, Brahmans, and Israelites, indeed in their knowledge that of the Christian religion, without which you would never know how to evaluate the high worth of the Gospels properly."

With this turn the faces of the clergymen, which had been directed rigidly at the speaker up to then, brightened up, and each now felt, since they now saw themselves at once transported into their subject, forced to say something. One said you could not predict in what relation the Bible overall or the Gospels stand to such an archetypal doctrine of language. Another claimed that not a single trace which pointed to such a doctrine was to be found particularly in the latter. Each presented their objections, and they already thought they had driven their opponent into a corner when he asked for a few minutes for a response and said, "The honoured company has attacked me with combined forces when I dared onto their territory, in order to force my retreat; but precisely the Bible, and particularly the New Testament, delivers indubitable proof of such a universal doctrine in which we are obliged to enter. When we hear in this respect firstly Christ himself, when he speaks with Peter and addresses him almost every time with a different name. Anyone who understands the doctrine of forms that has just been presented is easily able to comprehends the cause of this change of name. But the Revelation of John speaks for it more clearly than anything where Christ says, "I am Alpha and Omega, the first and the last."* One relates these words indeed only analogically to the Greek alphabet, where A is the first and O is the last letter. But precisely in this lies the extent of the entire interpretation in that Christ thereby says himself: "I am the entire alphabet." I could cite yet a number of individual places which refer to this topic, but these few may suffice, all the more as I can yet add that those who are incapable of grasping it or of believing it should make the attempt, whereby they will certainly obtain the most evidential proof."

The listeners felt so moved both by the matter and also by the certainty of the presentation that they declared they considered themselves indeed not yet vanquished, but so weakened that they would have to ask for an armistice. This suggestion was naturally accepted and brought a toast for the Doctor. He thanked them for it and asked for forgiveness that

---

*   [Tr.: cf. Revelation 22:13: "I am Alpha and Omega, the beginning and the end, the first and the last."]

he had stepped a little too close to their position; only it was now just his way to not be able to stay silent when he had to speak in the name of an eternal truth.

The time came to go home. The clergymen had obtained such a reverence for the Doctor that they accompanied him to the carriage and regarded themselves lucky to be able to yet do him an honour. He and Gomphardt travelled back to the town and gave the Professor that day a report of what had been said. The latter exclaimed highly satisfied, "So should all freemasons work, then we would have hope of gathering all humanity into our temple."

***

Gomphardt and the Professor were preparing themselves for their departure. It was already the 17th of September and they had resolved to start on the 20th because the Professor wanted to visit a few towns and as a mineralogist get to know the types of stone of those regions more closely. Almarkus needed no preparation; he pushed his departure out to the 25th because he did not intend lingering anywhere and was accustomed to travelling by day and night. When his two friends took their leave from him on the day of their departure, he said, "Happy travels! On the 1st of October we will see each other again at Gomphardt's estate at lunchtime. You can certainly count on me arriving at the proper time, just before the soup gets cold. Here I must visit a few patients and have myself paid by those who have become well."

His friends climbed into the carriage and went away under the sound of the post horn.

Gomphardt then arrived on the 29th September with the Professor at his estate. Doctor Reiner had arrived two days earlier, accompanied by Captain von Glückhof, one of his most loyal followers and friends. He had sought to make the acquaintance of the Deacon and had found all the good things which Gomphardt had said about this venerable clergyman to be justified to the fullest extent. The latter had let him read the letters of the Professor and obtained thereby a pleasure and an instruction which he had had no hope of ever re-ceiving in his life. Gimper had also already arrived, but by virtue of his peculiarities not got involved in any closer discussion, neither with Reiner, nor with the Deacon. Thus, with the exception of Doctor Almarkus, the entire company had assembled, and each sought either to rejoice in the reunion, or to have news given about the results of the various activities.

Gomphardt, who had found his property in the best of states, had thanked his administrator and instructed him to organise a party for all the servants on the 1st of October and to take care of its being carried out.

The 1st of October was almost half over. The midday meal was arranged, but still the seventh guest was missing. "Who shall take the chair?", Gomphardt asked. Reiner answered, "The Deacon." The latter refused such a distinction, because he did not possess enough adroitness for it, and suggested the Professor. Since he too refused, Gomphardt said, "So the still awaited guest shall take the chair and lead the discussion of our little circle. After the completed meal everyone will then confess that the chair was preferred to him, and that we would have been so highly edified under no other leadership.

The hand of the clock moved ever closer to the hour of one o'clock, and still the awaited guest was missing. It struck one on the tower clock. At the same moment the post horn blared, and Almarkus drove in a sharp trot to the house. Gomphardt hurried down to receive him, accompanied him to his room, and then led him by his hand to the dining room. All eyes were riveted on the arrival, and Gimper, who was standing by the window, barely trusted his eyes; finally he asked whether he was dreaming then, or whether the dead had arisen?

Everybody looked now at Gimper, who was still standing motionless by the window.

"Gimper!", Almarkus cried out.

"Master," he said.

"Come to me."

"May I?"

"Rascal, does your conscience oppress you?"

"It will oppress me to the ground if you do not support me."

He approached Almarkus as if he wanted to sink down before him. Almarkus held him upright and said, "Be calm! All is forgiven. What I left behind to you in Paris remains your property." — "Master," Gimper replied, "that is not right.

I have kept it for you, and to the extent you do not need it, surely you have relatives." — "Nobody," answered Almarkus, "but a sister who, if she does die before me, will make me richer by at least about sixty thousand talers. Thus not a word more about it. Now we want to go to the table and enjoy being gathered in such a beautiful circle."

They sat down, and indeed Almarkus at the head; the Professor and Reiner sat opposite him, to the right the Deacon and Gomphardt, to the left the Captain and Gimper. They dined well and with a pleasant mood, the best spice of any meal. After the main meal was over, the dessert was brought out and the table provided with wine, Gomphardt had the servants leave and not enter again before they were needed.

Deep silence reigned. Each felt that it would be difficult for them to have to speak even a few words without disturbing the prevailing mood. Almarkus, who in such moments seemed to feel the innermost driving force of his life, rejoiced in such a rare moment and finally interrupted the silence in that he asked the company to fill their glasses in order to drink a toast to the return of the owner of the house. Everybody obeyed this request and he began.

"In the name of all who awaited you here with love, our friend and brother, and have received you with love; in the name of the sacred penates* which reside in your house; in the remembrance of all that which you possess here, which you feel here, which you have loved and lost and are convinced you will find again; in the consciousness of a refound life, of an unwavering love and a blissful freedom of the spirit, I greet you on your property and empty to such an end this glass to the dregs."

Everybody enthusiastically drank their welcome to the returned houseowner.

Gomphardt asked to be permitted to give thanks for this welcome, stood up and said, "What I lost here, everybody knows. To what desperate steps my loss led me too, you know likewise. With what wealth I now return, I must not even say, since you all know how to appreciate the fullness of it. But

---

*   [Tr.: penates were household gods of Roman religion.]

whom do I thank for this wealth? — Firstly our reverend and very worthy Deacon, who preserved me from all temptation through the tie with which he bound me to himself, and put in my hand a secure rudder against the storms of life by virtue of which I did not have to rest until I had recognised the safe haven. To him I firstly drink my thanks.

By means of this rudder I found a place of anchor in the vicinity of my dear friend and brother Reiner, who showed me with sharp contours the goal of life, the goal of reason and of the spirit, in a word, the basic need of humanity. To him I owe the firmness on the resulting odysseys of my journey and the certainty with which I could recognise all the enticements and shallows and evade them. To him, this strong spirit who without prospect of reward, true to his decision once made, did not give up hope and waver and was to me an example of manly persistence, to him my thanks and my admiration.

Fate led me to the haven, to the hands of my teacher and friend, Professor Rückmann. What he was and gave to me, I cannot describe with words. He gave me life, freedom, the confidence of existence, in a word, the certainty that there is no separation, but rather an eternal remaining in existence, an eternal life in each other and for each other and the conviction that the sting of death can well wound, but not kill.

I must drink one more toast to our friend and brother, Doctor Almarkus. He came to us like a shooting star which illuminates humanity on its own paths. He gave us the example of *how highly and gloriously freemasonry can reward its adherents when they do not become disloyal to it, seek only in its symbols and use them everywhere where your steps take you to spread light and truth!* He is a hero who vanquishes with irresistible power every obstacle and strikes the enemy of darkness with strong weapons to the ground. He is the free man who devotes himself not with humble demeanour, but with clear brow to the truth, his friend. He is the light which taught me manliness in the struggle for genuine wisdom and gave me courage to seek and to find it in all life circumstances. I lack the power to worthily describe the genius which resides in him and guides him, and hence I can state nothing more than: I praise the hour which brought him to us, and this feeling will never leave me as long as I think and feel."

He emptied his glass to the dregs, and everybody solemnly agreed with him, their marvelling looks directed at Almarkus.

The Deacon, who felt powerfully edified by all he had seen and heard here, desired to speak, and expressed himself in the following way.

"According to the spirit I feel at home amongst you, but according to the form still estranged, hence I will limit myself to a few words.

With sadness I saw five years ago our friend Gomphardt part from this district. But at the time already despite the grief a light shone in my heart which told me: he will return richer than he left. My suspicion has been fulfilled, and I can do nothing but express to the friends which accepted him so faithfully my most intimate thanks and ask the creator to bless them for what they have done with the fullness of his grace and to send them everything which their noble hearts consider desirable."

Everybody endeavoured to elevate this glorious celebration through maxims and talks; even Gimper joined in and declared that he would not in future summon any spirits, but instead strive to seek his own spirit from which according to the testimony of those brothers present alone comes true knowledge.

When a pause occurred, the Captain asked to speak and said, "You will forgive me when I, as it were an uninvited guest, allow myself to speak here too. What I have heard in this circle is so uplifting of the heart that I wish every genuine freemason could have taken part in it. Only whom have we to thank for these precious moments? Without offending any guest, it clearly follows that without the effective and instructive spirit of our brother Rückmann we could never have found ourselves together in this way. He has freed our friend Gomphardt from the uncertainty and given a light to him, the animating rays of which have also enlightened us and shown us the only way to truth. Through him we have come into contact with our enlightened brother Almarkus. He has won the reverend Deacon over to our cause and thereby shown that our doctrine is not tied up with any arbitrary institution. It is he to whom we owe everything in this regard, and hence I call on you to support me, and to offer him a toast of our thanks and our honest veneration."

Everybody agreed joyfully, and Almarkus said the effect of his brother Rückmann often occurred to him to be like the effect of the spirit of God which flows quietly everywhere and yet leads everything to its goal.

It was now time to conclude the festivities and to digest properly what had been enjoyed physically and spiritually. Almarkus, to whom this function fell as presiding chair, stood up, asked for a few moments for the attention of the honoured guests and said, "If in every town a circle were to be formed like we have here, then in a short time all the contention would have to vanish from the earth, and wisdom and peace would have to set up their banner. Since this cannot be, I ask all those present, especially the brother freemasons, to not hide their light under a bushel, but to let it shine. The great reproach which one made of the superiors of Catholicism in former times consisted in that they did not reveal their rituals, the Bible. We are hiding behind iron bars whilst we are chiding them. In our time the press has obtained rulership and draws everything into the light which serves humanity, which it has of the great and good. Free-masonry cannot withstand this rule, it must bring its matter into the daylight, otherwise it will subside, in that it evades the reigning control, into itself and will in a short time barely still exist as a lifeless mummy. The foundation of the temple of freemasonry has been laid; now humanity must see its labours. With twelve witnesses Christ called his religion to life, here there are six. If we do not remain idle, we must succeed in growing to twelve and preparing a new day for the world where the primal truth walks hand in hand with religion, where one holds and strengthens the other, where all humans, driven by the spirit and its voice which resides in us, walk the straight path and reach their high destiny. With this prospect we will end today's festivities, but will remain connected by our hearts in time and eternity. Amen."

***

**Other works by Johann Baptist Krebs
(originally published in German under
the pseudonym of J. B. Kerning)
published by K A Nitz**

Paths to Immortality
Based on the Undeniable Powers
of Human Nature

Christianity
or
God and Nature Only One
Through the Word

The Missionaries
The Path to the Teaching Profession
of Christianity

The Principles of the Bible

Wisdom of the Orient

And by his student Karl Kolb

The Rebirth, the inner true life, or
how do humans become blessed?
In accordance with the words of the sacred scripture
and the laws of thinking